50 Russian Tea Party Recipes for Home

By: Kelly Johnson

Table of Contents

- Blini with Sour Cream and Caviar
- Pelmeni (Russian Dumplings) with Sour Cream
- Russian Tea Cakes (Pryaniki)
- Olivier Salad (Russian Potato Salad)
- Beef Stroganoff
- Borscht (Beet Soup) with Sour Cream
- Selyodka Pod Shuboy (Layered Herring Salad)
- Piroshki (Stuffed Buns)
- Sharlotka (Russian Apple Cake)
- Sushki (Russian Tea Cookies)
- Kulebyaka (Russian Fish Pie)
- Chicken Kotleti (Russian Chicken Patties)
- Shchi (Cabbage Soup)
- Kartoshka (Russian Chocolate Potato Cake)
- Golubtsy (Stuffed Cabbage Rolls)
- Kvass (Russian Fermented Drink)
- Syrniki (Russian Cottage Cheese Pancakes)
- Medovik (Russian Honey Cake)
- Okroshka (Cold Summer Soup)
- Kartoshka (Russian Chocolate Truffles)
- Vatrushka (Russian Sweet Cheese Buns)
- Solyanka (Russian Meat and Pickle Soup)
- Tvorog (Russian Farmer's Cheese)
- Sirniki (Russian Farmer's Cheese Pancakes)
- Zapekanka (Russian Baked Cheesecake)
- Zavtrak (Russian Breakfast Pancakes)
- Uzvar (Russian Dried Fruit Compote)
- Kasha (Russian Porridge)
- Guriev Kasha (Russian Buckwheat Porridge)
- Russian Meatballs in Tomato Sauce
- Russian Black Bread (Pumpernickel)
- Russian Tea Samovar
- Rassolnik (Russian Pickle Soup)
- Kompot (Russian Fruit Punch)
- Russian Beef and Mushroom Stew

- Pryanik (Russian Honey-Spice Cake)
- Russkaya Salat (Russian Salad)
- Russkaya Ribka (Russian Fish Pie)
- Russian Mushroom and Potato Soup
- Russian Eggplant Caviar (Ikra)
- Russian Pickled Vegetables (Selyoniy)
- Russian Beet Salad (Vinegret)
- Russian Chicken Soup (Solyanka)
- Russian Cabbage Rolls (Golubtsy)
- Russian Mushroom Piroshki
- Russian Cabbage Pie (Kulebyaka)
- Russian Fish Soup (Ukha)
- Russian Garlic Bread (Pampushki)
- Russian Potato Pancakes (Draniki)
- Russian Meat Pie (Kurnik)

Blini with Sour Cream and Caviar

Ingredients:

For the Blini:

- 1 cup all-purpose flour
- 1 cup milk
- 1 large egg
- 1 tablespoon melted butter
- 1/2 teaspoon baking powder
- Pinch of salt
- Butter or oil for cooking

For Serving:

- Sour cream
- Caviar (salmon, sturgeon, or any preferred variety)
- Chopped fresh chives or dill (optional, for garnish)

Instructions:

Prepare the Blini Batter:
- In a mixing bowl, whisk together the flour, milk, egg, melted butter, baking powder, and a pinch of salt until smooth and well combined.
- Let the batter rest for about 15-20 minutes to allow the flour to hydrate and the batter to thicken slightly.

Cook the Blini:
- Heat a non-stick skillet or griddle over medium heat.
- Lightly grease the skillet with butter or oil.
- Pour a small amount of batter onto the skillet, using about 2 tablespoons for each blin. Use the back of a spoon to spread the batter into a thin, even circle.
- Cook the blini for 1-2 minutes on the first side, or until bubbles form on the surface and the edges begin to lift.
- Flip the blini and cook for an additional 1-2 minutes on the other side, or until golden brown and cooked through.
- Repeat the process with the remaining batter, greasing the skillet as needed.

Assemble the Blini:

- Once all the blini are cooked, transfer them to a serving platter.
- Spread a dollop of sour cream onto each blin.
- Top each blin with a small spoonful of caviar.

Serve:
- Garnish the blini with chopped fresh chives or dill, if desired.
- Arrange the blini on a platter and serve immediately, while still warm.
- Enjoy the luxurious combination of soft blini, creamy sour cream, and briny caviar!

Blini with sour cream and caviar are elegant and flavorful appetizers that are sure to impress your guests. Serve them as part of a Russian-themed party or as a sophisticated addition to any gathering or celebration.

Pelmeni (Russian Dumplings) with Sour Cream

Ingredients:

For the Pelmeni Dough:

- 2 cups all-purpose flour
- 1/2 teaspoon salt
- 1 large egg
- 1/2 cup water

For the Pelmeni Filling:

- 1/2 pound ground beef
- 1/2 pound ground pork
- 1 small onion, finely chopped
- 2 cloves garlic, minced
- Salt and black pepper to taste

For Serving:

- Sour cream
- Chopped fresh parsley or dill (optional, for garnish)

Instructions:

Make the Pelmeni Dough:
- In a large mixing bowl, combine the all-purpose flour and salt.
- Make a well in the center of the flour mixture and add the egg and water.
- Using a fork, gradually incorporate the flour into the wet ingredients until a dough forms.
- Knead the dough on a lightly floured surface for about 5-7 minutes, or until smooth and elastic.
- Wrap the dough in plastic wrap and let it rest at room temperature for about 30 minutes.

Prepare the Pelmeni Filling:
- In a separate mixing bowl, combine the ground beef, ground pork, finely chopped onion, minced garlic, salt, and black pepper.
- Mix until all the ingredients are well incorporated.

Assemble the Pelmeni:
- On a lightly floured surface, roll out the dough into a thin sheet, about 1/8 inch thick.
- Use a round cookie cutter or a glass to cut out circles from the dough.
- Place a small spoonful of the filling in the center of each dough circle.
- Fold the dough over the filling to form a half-moon shape, then pinch the edges together to seal.

Cook the Pelmeni:
- Bring a large pot of salted water to a boil.
- Carefully drop the pelmeni into the boiling water, working in batches to avoid overcrowding the pot.
- Cook the pelmeni for about 5-7 minutes, or until they float to the surface and are cooked through.

Serve:
- Use a slotted spoon to transfer the cooked pelmeni to serving plates.
- Serve the pelmeni hot, with a dollop of sour cream on top.
- Garnish with chopped fresh parsley or dill, if desired.
- Enjoy the delicious and comforting pelmeni with sour cream!

Pelmeni with sour cream are a classic Russian comfort food dish that's perfect for a cozy dinner or gathering with friends and family. The combination of tender dumplings and creamy sour cream is sure to warm your soul.

Russian Tea Cakes (Pryaniki)

Ingredients:

- 2 cups all-purpose flour
- 1/2 cup granulated sugar
- 1/2 cup unsalted butter, softened
- 1 large egg
- 1/4 cup honey
- 1 teaspoon baking soda
- 1 teaspoon ground cinnamon
- 1/2 teaspoon ground ginger
- 1/4 teaspoon ground cloves
- Pinch of salt
- Powdered sugar, for dusting

Instructions:

Preheat the Oven:
- Preheat your oven to 350°F (175°C). Line a baking sheet with parchment paper or lightly grease it.

Prepare the Dough:
- In a mixing bowl, cream together the softened butter and granulated sugar until light and fluffy.
- Add the egg and honey to the butter-sugar mixture, and mix until well combined.

Combine Dry Ingredients:
- In a separate bowl, whisk together the all-purpose flour, baking soda, ground cinnamon, ground ginger, ground cloves, and a pinch of salt.

Mix the Dough:
- Gradually add the dry ingredients to the wet ingredients, mixing until a soft dough forms. You may need to use your hands to knead the dough until it comes together.

Shape the Cookies:
- Pinch off small portions of dough and roll them into balls, about 1 inch in diameter. Place the dough balls on the prepared baking sheet, spacing them a couple of inches apart.

Bake:
- Bake the cookies in the preheated oven for 10-12 minutes, or until they are lightly golden brown around the edges.

Cool and Dust:
- Allow the cookies to cool on the baking sheet for a few minutes before transferring them to a wire rack to cool completely.
- Once the cookies are cool, dust them generously with powdered sugar.

Serve:
- Serve the Russian tea cakes (pryaniki) with a cup of hot tea or coffee, and enjoy their deliciously tender texture and warming spices!

These Russian tea cakes (pryaniki) are perfect for holiday gatherings, afternoon tea, or any time you crave a sweet and comforting treat. Store any leftovers in an airtight container for up to a week. Enjoy!

Olivier Salad (Russian Potato Salad)

Ingredients:

- 3 large potatoes, peeled and diced
- 2 carrots, peeled and diced
- 4 eggs
- 1 cup frozen peas, thawed
- 1 cup diced cooked ham or bologna (optional)
- 1/2 cup diced pickles (dill or sweet)
- 1/2 cup diced cooked chicken or boiled beef (optional)
- 1/2 cup diced apple (optional)
- 1/4 cup diced onion (red or yellow)
- 1/2 cup mayonnaise
- 2 tablespoons Dijon mustard
- Salt and pepper to taste
- Chopped fresh dill or parsley for garnish (optional)

Instructions:

Cook Potatoes and Carrots:
- Place the diced potatoes and carrots in a pot of salted water.
- Bring to a boil and cook until tender, about 10-15 minutes.
- Drain and let cool.

Cook Eggs:
- Place the eggs in a pot and cover with water.
- Bring to a boil over medium heat.
- Once boiling, remove from heat, cover, and let the eggs sit in the hot water for 10-12 minutes.
- Drain and cool the eggs under cold running water, then peel and chop them.

Assemble the Salad:
- In a large mixing bowl, combine the cooked potatoes, carrots, chopped eggs, thawed peas, diced ham or bologna (if using), diced pickles, diced chicken or beef (if using), diced apple (if using), and diced onion.
- In a small bowl, whisk together the mayonnaise and Dijon mustard until well combined.
- Pour the dressing over the salad ingredients and gently toss until everything is evenly coated.
- Season with salt and pepper to taste.

Chill and Serve:
- Cover the salad and refrigerate for at least 1 hour to allow the flavors to meld.
- Before serving, garnish with chopped fresh dill or parsley, if desired.
- Serve chilled as a side dish or appetizer.

Enjoy this hearty and delicious Olivier Salad (Russian Potato Salad) with your favorite main dishes or as a standalone meal. It's perfect for gatherings, potlucks, or any time you're craving a taste of Russian cuisine!

Beef Stroganoff

Ingredients:

- 1 lb (450g) beef sirloin or tenderloin, thinly sliced
- Salt and pepper to taste
- 2 tablespoons olive oil
- 1 onion, finely chopped
- 2 cloves garlic, minced
- 8 oz (225g) mushrooms, sliced
- 2 tablespoons all-purpose flour
- 1 cup beef broth
- 1 tablespoon Worcestershire sauce
- 1 cup sour cream
- 2 tablespoons Dijon mustard
- 1 tablespoon paprika
- Chopped fresh parsley, for garnish (optional)
- Cooked egg noodles or rice, for serving

Instructions:

Prepare the Beef:
- Season the thinly sliced beef with salt and pepper.
- Heat 1 tablespoon of olive oil in a large skillet over medium-high heat.
- Add the beef slices to the skillet and cook for 2-3 minutes per side, until browned. Remove the beef from the skillet and set aside.

Cook the Onion, Garlic, and Mushrooms:
- In the same skillet, add the remaining tablespoon of olive oil.
- Add the chopped onion and minced garlic to the skillet and sauté for 2-3 minutes, until softened.
- Add the sliced mushrooms to the skillet and cook for an additional 5-6 minutes, until they release their juices and become tender.

Make the Sauce:
- Sprinkle the flour over the mushrooms and onions in the skillet. Stir to combine and cook for 1-2 minutes.
- Gradually pour in the beef broth, stirring constantly to prevent lumps from forming.
- Stir in the Worcestershire sauce, Dijon mustard, and paprika.
- Reduce the heat to low and simmer the sauce for 5-7 minutes, until thickened.

Finish the Dish:
- Return the cooked beef slices to the skillet, along with any juices that have accumulated.
- Stir in the sour cream, mixing until well combined.
- Cook for an additional 2-3 minutes, until the beef is heated through and the sauce is creamy.
- Taste and adjust seasoning with salt and pepper if needed.

Serve:
- Serve the Beef Stroganoff hot over cooked egg noodles or rice.
- Garnish with chopped fresh parsley, if desired.
- Enjoy this comforting and flavorful dish!

Beef Stroganoff is a hearty and satisfying meal that's perfect for cozy dinners or special occasions. The creamy sauce and tender beef pair perfectly with the pasta or rice.

Borscht (Beet Soup) with Sour Cream

Ingredients:

- 2 tablespoons olive oil or vegetable oil
- 1 onion, finely chopped
- 2 carrots, peeled and diced
- 2 stalks celery, diced
- 2 medium beets, peeled and grated
- 2 potatoes, peeled and diced
- 4 cups vegetable or beef broth
- 1 can (14 oz) diced tomatoes
- 2 tablespoons tomato paste
- 2 cloves garlic, minced
- 1 bay leaf
- 1 teaspoon dried dill (or 1 tablespoon fresh dill, chopped)
- Salt and pepper to taste
- 1 tablespoon red wine vinegar (optional)
- Sour cream, for serving
- Chopped fresh dill, for garnish (optional)

Instructions:

Sauté the Vegetables:
- Heat the olive oil in a large pot over medium heat.
- Add the chopped onion, diced carrots, and diced celery to the pot. Sauté for 5-6 minutes, until the vegetables are softened.

Add Beets and Potatoes:
- Add the grated beets and diced potatoes to the pot. Stir to combine with the sautéed vegetables.

Add Broth and Tomatoes:
- Pour in the vegetable or beef broth and add the diced tomatoes (with their juices).
- Stir in the tomato paste, minced garlic, bay leaf, and dried dill. Season with salt and pepper to taste.

Simmer:
- Bring the soup to a simmer over medium-low heat. Cover and cook for 30-40 minutes, or until the vegetables are tender.

Adjust Seasoning:

- Taste the soup and adjust seasoning with salt, pepper, and red wine vinegar (if using). The vinegar adds a tangy flavor that balances the sweetness of the beets.

Serve:
- Ladle the hot borscht into serving bowls.
- Serve each bowl with a dollop of sour cream and a sprinkle of chopped fresh dill, if desired.
- Enjoy this hearty and comforting borscht with sour cream!

Borscht is a nutritious and satisfying soup that's perfect for chilly days. The addition of sour cream adds a creamy texture and tangy flavor that complements the earthy sweetness of the beets. Serve it as a starter or as a main course with crusty bread on the side.

Selyodka Pod Shuboy (Layered Herring Salad)

Ingredients:

- 2 large potatoes, boiled and thinly sliced
- 2 medium beets, boiled and thinly sliced
- 2 large carrots, boiled and thinly sliced
- 1 large onion, thinly sliced
- 4-6 pickled herring fillets, cut into small pieces
- 1 cup mayonnaise
- Salt and pepper to taste
- Chopped fresh dill, for garnish (optional)

Instructions:

Prepare the Ingredients:
- Boil the potatoes, beets, and carrots until they are tender. Allow them to cool, then peel and thinly slice them.
- Thinly slice the onion.

Assemble the Salad:
- Start by placing a layer of sliced potatoes on the bottom of a serving dish.
- Top the potatoes with a layer of sliced beets, followed by a layer of sliced carrots, and finally a layer of sliced onions.
- Arrange the pickled herring pieces on top of the onions.

Repeat the Layers:
- Repeat the layers of potatoes, beets, carrots, onions, and herring until all the ingredients are used, ending with a layer of onions and herring on top.

Add Mayonnaise:
- Spread a generous amount of mayonnaise over the top layer of onions and herring, covering the entire surface of the salad.

Chill and Serve:
- Cover the salad with plastic wrap and refrigerate for at least 2-3 hours, or overnight, to allow the flavors to meld.
- Before serving, garnish the salad with chopped fresh dill, if desired.
- Slice and serve the Selyodka Pod Shuboy chilled, as a delightful appetizer or side dish.

This Layered Herring Salad is a classic Russian dish that's perfect for special occasions or gatherings. The combination of tender potatoes, sweet beets, flavorful herring, and creamy mayonnaise creates a harmonious and delicious flavor profile. Enjoy!

Piroshki (Stuffed Buns)

Ingredients:

For the Dough:

- 2 cups all-purpose flour
- 1/2 cup warm milk
- 1/4 cup warm water
- 2 tablespoons unsalted butter, melted
- 1 tablespoon granulated sugar
- 1 teaspoon active dry yeast
- 1/2 teaspoon salt
- 1 egg, beaten (for egg wash)

For the Filling:

- 1 cup cooked and seasoned ground meat (beef, pork, or chicken)
- 1 small onion, finely chopped
- 1 medium potato, boiled and mashed
- 1 carrot, grated
- Salt and pepper to taste
- Oil for frying

Instructions:

Prepare the Dough:
- In a small bowl, combine the warm milk, warm water, sugar, and yeast. Let it sit for about 5-10 minutes until frothy.
- In a large mixing bowl, combine the flour and salt. Make a well in the center and pour in the yeast mixture and melted butter.
- Mix until a dough forms. Knead the dough on a floured surface for about 5-7 minutes until smooth and elastic.
- Place the dough in a greased bowl, cover with a clean kitchen towel, and let it rise in a warm place for about 1 hour or until doubled in size.

Prepare the Filling:
- In a skillet, heat some oil over medium heat. Add the chopped onion and grated carrot and cook until softened.

- Add the cooked ground meat and mashed potato to the skillet. Season with salt and pepper to taste. Cook for a few minutes until heated through. Remove from heat and let it cool.

Assemble the Piroshki:
- Punch down the risen dough and divide it into small balls, about the size of a golf ball.
- Roll out each ball into a circle on a floured surface. Place a spoonful of the filling in the center of each circle.
- Fold the edges of the dough over the filling to enclose it and form a bun. Pinch the edges to seal.

Fry the Piroshki:
- Heat oil in a deep skillet or pot over medium heat.
- Gently place the stuffed buns in the hot oil, seam side down. Fry until golden brown on all sides, turning as needed, about 3-4 minutes per side.
- Remove the fried piroshki from the oil and place them on a paper towel-lined plate to drain excess oil.

Serve:
- Serve the piroshki hot, as a delicious appetizer or snack. They can be enjoyed on their own or with a side of sour cream or dipping sauce.

These homemade piroshki are flavorful, comforting, and perfect for sharing with family and friends. Feel free to experiment with different fillings to suit your taste preferences.

Enjoy!

Sharlotka (Russian Apple Cake)

Ingredients:

- 4 large apples, peeled, cored, and thinly sliced
- 3 large eggs
- 1 cup granulated sugar
- 1 cup all-purpose flour
- 1 teaspoon baking powder
- 1/4 teaspoon salt
- 1 teaspoon vanilla extract
- Powdered sugar, for dusting (optional)
- Fresh berries or whipped cream, for serving (optional)

Instructions:

Preheat the Oven:
- Preheat your oven to 350°F (175°C). Grease a 9-inch (23 cm) round cake pan and line the bottom with parchment paper.

Prepare the Apples:
- Peel, core, and thinly slice the apples. Set aside.

Make the Batter:
- In a large mixing bowl, beat the eggs and sugar together until pale and fluffy.
- Add the vanilla extract and mix until combined.
- In a separate bowl, sift together the flour, baking powder, and salt.
- Gradually add the dry ingredients to the egg mixture, mixing until just combined.

Assemble the Cake:
- Gently fold the sliced apples into the batter until evenly coated.
- Pour the batter into the prepared cake pan, spreading it out evenly.

Bake:
- Bake the cake in the preheated oven for 40-45 minutes, or until golden brown and a toothpick inserted into the center comes out clean.

Cool and Serve:
- Allow the cake to cool in the pan for about 10 minutes, then carefully remove it from the pan and transfer it to a wire rack to cool completely.
- Once cooled, dust the top of the cake with powdered sugar, if desired.
- Slice and serve the Sharlotka with fresh berries or whipped cream, if desired.

Enjoy:
- Serve the Russian Apple Cake slices warm or at room temperature, and enjoy the delicious flavors of tender apples and delicate cake!

Sharlotka is a beloved Russian dessert that's perfect for any occasion. Its simplicity and comforting taste make it a favorite among both kids and adults. Enjoy!

Sushki (Russian Tea Cookies)

Ingredients:

- 2 cups all-purpose flour
- 1/2 cup granulated sugar
- 1/2 teaspoon baking powder
- 1/4 teaspoon salt
- 1/2 cup unsalted butter, softened
- 2 large eggs
- 1 teaspoon vanilla extract
- Optional toppings: poppy seeds, sesame seeds, chopped nuts

Instructions:

Preheat the Oven:
- Preheat your oven to 350°F (175°C). Line a baking sheet with parchment paper.

Prepare the Dough:
- In a mixing bowl, sift together the flour, sugar, baking powder, and salt.
- Add the softened butter to the dry ingredients and mix until crumbly.

Add Wet Ingredients:
- Beat the eggs lightly and add them to the bowl along with the vanilla extract.
- Mix until the dough comes together. It should be firm but not too sticky. If it's too dry, you can add a little milk or water, a teaspoon at a time.

Shape the Cookies:
- Pinch off small pieces of dough and roll them into ropes about 4 inches long and 1/2 inch thick.
- Bring the ends of each rope together and press them firmly to form a ring or bagel shape.

Optional Toppings:
- If desired, you can brush the tops of the sushki with a little water and sprinkle them with poppy seeds, sesame seeds, or chopped nuts.

Bake:
- Place the shaped cookies on the prepared baking sheet, leaving a little space between each one.
- Bake in the preheated oven for 12-15 minutes, or until lightly golden brown.

Cool:

- Remove the sushki from the oven and let them cool on the baking sheet for a few minutes before transferring them to a wire rack to cool completely.

Serve:
- Once cooled, sushki are ready to be served. Enjoy them with a cup of tea or coffee, or as a snack any time of day.

These homemade sushki are a delightful treat with their crunchy texture and subtle sweetness. They are perfect for enjoying with your favorite hot beverage or as a snack on their own. Enjoy!

Kulebyaka (Russian Fish Pie)

Ingredients:

For the Dough:

- 2 1/2 cups all-purpose flour
- 1 cup unsalted butter, chilled and cubed
- 1/2 cup sour cream
- 1/2 teaspoon salt

For the Filling:

- 1 lb (450g) firm white fish fillets (such as cod or haddock), diced
- 1 cup cooked rice
- 4 hard-boiled eggs, chopped
- 1 onion, finely chopped
- 8 oz (225g) mushrooms, sliced
- 2 tablespoons butter
- Salt and pepper to taste
- 1 tablespoon fresh dill, chopped
- 1 tablespoon fresh parsley, chopped
- 1 egg, beaten (for egg wash)

Instructions:

Prepare the Dough:
- In a large mixing bowl, combine the flour and salt. Add the chilled cubed butter and use a pastry cutter or your fingers to cut the butter into the flour until the mixture resembles coarse crumbs.
- Add the sour cream and mix until the dough comes together. Shape the dough into a ball, wrap it in plastic wrap, and refrigerate for at least 30 minutes.

Prepare the Filling:
- In a skillet, melt the butter over medium heat. Add the chopped onion and sauté until softened.
- Add the sliced mushrooms to the skillet and cook until they release their juices and become tender.
- Add the diced fish fillets to the skillet and cook until they are just cooked through. Season with salt and pepper to taste.

- Remove the skillet from heat and stir in the cooked rice, chopped hard-boiled eggs, fresh dill, and fresh parsley. Let the filling cool slightly.

Assemble the Pie:

- Preheat your oven to 375°F (190°C). Line a baking sheet with parchment paper.
- Roll out two-thirds of the chilled dough on a floured surface to fit the bottom and sides of a greased 9-inch (23 cm) pie dish.
- Spoon the cooled fish and rice filling into the prepared pie dish, spreading it out evenly.
- Roll out the remaining dough and place it over the filling to cover the pie. Seal the edges and trim any excess dough. Cut a few slits in the top crust to allow steam to escape.
- Brush the top of the pie with beaten egg for a golden finish.

Bake:

- Place the pie dish on the prepared baking sheet and bake in the preheated oven for 40-45 minutes, or until the crust is golden brown and cooked through.

Serve:

- Remove the pie from the oven and let it cool for a few minutes before slicing.
- Serve the Kulebyaka warm, with a side salad or your favorite sauce.

This Russian Fish Pie is a delicious and comforting dish that's perfect for a special occasion or family dinner. Enjoy the layers of flaky pastry and flavorful filling in every bite!

Chicken Kotleti (Russian Chicken Patties)

Ingredients:

- 1 lb (450g) ground chicken
- 1 small onion, finely chopped
- 1-2 cloves garlic, minced
- 1/4 cup breadcrumbs
- 1 egg
- 1 tablespoon mayonnaise
- 1 teaspoon Dijon mustard
- 1 teaspoon Worcestershire sauce
- 1 teaspoon dried herbs (such as dill, parsley, or thyme)
- Salt and pepper to taste
- Oil for frying

Instructions:

Prepare the Ingredients:
- In a mixing bowl, combine the ground chicken, finely chopped onion, minced garlic, breadcrumbs, egg, mayonnaise, Dijon mustard, Worcestershire sauce, dried herbs, salt, and pepper.

Mix the Ingredients:
- Use your hands or a spoon to mix the ingredients until well combined. Be careful not to overmix, as this can make the patties tough.

Shape the Patties:
- Divide the mixture into equal portions and shape each portion into a patty. You can make them round or oval-shaped, whichever you prefer.

Cook the Patties:
- Heat oil in a skillet over medium heat.
- Once the oil is hot, add the patties to the skillet in batches, making sure not to overcrowd the pan.
- Cook the patties for 4-5 minutes on each side, or until they are golden brown and cooked through. The internal temperature should reach 165°F (74°C).

Serve:
- Once cooked, transfer the chicken kotleti to a plate lined with paper towels to drain any excess oil.
- Serve the chicken kotleti hot, with your favorite side dishes such as mashed potatoes, rice, or vegetables.

- Enjoy these flavorful and juicy Russian chicken patties as a comforting meal!

Chicken Kotleti are versatile and can be customized with different seasonings and herbs to suit your taste preferences. They are perfect for a family dinner or as a tasty snack. Enjoy!

Shchi (Cabbage Soup)

Ingredients:

- 1 small head of cabbage, shredded
- 2 carrots, peeled and diced
- 2 potatoes, peeled and diced
- 1 onion, finely chopped
- 2 cloves garlic, minced
- 1 bay leaf
- 6 cups vegetable or beef broth
- 2 tablespoons tomato paste
- 2 tablespoons vegetable oil
- Salt and pepper to taste
- Fresh dill or parsley for garnish (optional)
- Sour cream for serving (optional)

Instructions:

Sauté Vegetables:
- In a large soup pot, heat the vegetable oil over medium heat. Add the chopped onion and diced carrots, and sauté until softened, about 5 minutes.
- Add the minced garlic and cook for an additional 1-2 minutes, until fragrant.

Add Cabbage:
- Add the shredded cabbage to the pot and stir to combine with the onions and carrots. Cook for a few minutes until the cabbage starts to wilt.

Add Broth and Potatoes:
- Pour the vegetable or beef broth into the pot, along with the bay leaf and tomato paste. Stir well.
- Add the diced potatoes to the pot and bring the soup to a simmer.

Simmer:
- Reduce the heat to low and let the soup simmer, partially covered, for about 20-25 minutes, or until the vegetables are tender.

Season and Serve:
- Taste the soup and season with salt and pepper to taste.
- Remove the bay leaf from the soup.
- Ladle the Shchi into serving bowls and garnish with fresh dill or parsley, if desired.

- Serve hot, with a dollop of sour cream on top if desired.

Shchi is a hearty and comforting soup that's perfect for cold weather. It's nutritious, flavorful, and easy to make with simple ingredients. Enjoy it as a starter or as a main course with bread on the side.

Kartoshka (Russian Chocolate Potato Cake)

Ingredients:

- 2 cups mashed potatoes (cooked and cooled)
- 1 cup crushed tea biscuits or graham crackers
- 1/2 cup unsweetened cocoa powder
- 1/2 cup powdered sugar
- 1/2 cup chopped nuts (optional)
- 1/4 cup dried fruit (such as raisins or cranberries) (optional)
- 1 teaspoon vanilla extract
- 1/2 cup unsalted butter, melted
- Chocolate glaze (optional):
    - 1/2 cup chocolate chips
    - 2 tablespoons unsalted butter

Instructions:

Prepare the Mashed Potatoes:
- Peel, dice, and boil potatoes until they are soft. Drain and mash them until smooth. Let them cool completely before using.

Mix Ingredients:
- In a large mixing bowl, combine the mashed potatoes, crushed biscuits, cocoa powder, powdered sugar, chopped nuts (if using), dried fruit (if using), vanilla extract, and melted butter.
- Mix all the ingredients together until well combined. The mixture should be thick and fudgy.

Shape the Cake:
- Take small portions of the mixture and shape them into small round or oval-shaped cakes, about the size of a golf ball.
- Place the shaped cakes on a baking sheet lined with parchment paper.

Chill:
- Place the baking sheet in the refrigerator and chill the cakes for at least 1-2 hours, or until they are firm.

Make the Chocolate Glaze (optional):
- In a microwave-safe bowl, combine the chocolate chips and butter. Microwave in 30-second intervals, stirring in between, until the chocolate is melted and smooth.

Glaze the Cakes (optional):

- Once the cakes are chilled and firm, dip each cake into the melted chocolate glaze to coat it evenly. Place the coated cakes back on the parchment-lined baking sheet.

Chill Again (optional):

- Return the baking sheet to the refrigerator and chill the cakes for an additional 30 minutes, or until the chocolate glaze is set.

Serve:

- Serve the Kartoshka cakes chilled as a delightful dessert or snack.

Kartoshka is a unique and decadent Russian dessert that's sure to impress your friends and family. Enjoy the rich chocolate flavor and soft texture of these delightful cakes!

Golubtsy (Stuffed Cabbage Rolls)

Ingredients:

For the Cabbage Rolls:

- 1 large head of cabbage
- 1 lb (450g) ground beef or pork
- 1/2 cup uncooked rice
- 1 onion, finely chopped
- 2 cloves garlic, minced
- 1 egg
- Salt and pepper to taste
- 1/4 cup chopped fresh dill (optional)
- 1/4 cup chopped fresh parsley (optional)

For the Tomato Sauce:

- 1 can (14 oz) crushed tomatoes
- 1 can (8 oz) tomato sauce
- 1 tablespoon tomato paste
- 1 onion, finely chopped
- 2 cloves garlic, minced
- 1 teaspoon sugar
- 1 teaspoon paprika
- Salt and pepper to taste

Instructions:

Prepare the Cabbage Leaves:
- Bring a large pot of water to a boil. Carefully remove the core from the cabbage and place the whole head in the boiling water.
- Cook for about 5-7 minutes, until the outer leaves are softened and can be easily peeled off. Remove the leaves and set them aside to cool.

Make the Filling:
- In a mixing bowl, combine the ground meat, uncooked rice, finely chopped onion, minced garlic, egg, salt, pepper, and chopped fresh herbs (if using). Mix until well combined.

Fill the Cabbage Leaves:

- Take one cabbage leaf and place a spoonful of the meat mixture in the center.
- Roll the leaf tightly around the filling, tucking in the sides as you go. Repeat with the remaining cabbage leaves and filling.

Prepare the Tomato Sauce:

- In a separate saucepan, heat a little oil over medium heat. Add the finely chopped onion and minced garlic, and sauté until softened.
- Add the crushed tomatoes, tomato sauce, tomato paste, sugar, paprika, salt, and pepper. Stir well to combine and simmer for about 5-7 minutes.

Cook the Golubtsy:

- Place the rolled cabbage leaves seam-side down in a large pot or Dutch oven.
- Pour the tomato sauce over the cabbage rolls, covering them completely.
- Cover the pot and simmer over low heat for about 45-60 minutes, or until the cabbage rolls are cooked through and the rice is tender.

Serve:

- Serve the Golubtsy hot, garnished with additional chopped fresh herbs if desired.
- Enjoy these delicious and comforting stuffed cabbage rolls as a main course!

Golubtsy are a hearty and satisfying dish that's perfect for a cozy family dinner or special occasion. The combination of tender cabbage, flavorful meat filling, and savory tomato sauce is sure to be a hit!

Kvass (Russian Fermented Drink)

Ingredients:

- 1 loaf of stale rye bread (about 1 lb or 450g)
- 4 quarts (4 liters) water
- 1 cup sugar
- 1/4 cup raisins (optional)
- 1 tablespoon active dry yeast

Instructions:

Prepare the Bread:
- Preheat your oven to 350°F (175°C). Cut the loaf of stale rye bread into cubes and spread them out on a baking sheet.
- Bake the bread cubes in the preheated oven for about 15-20 minutes, or until they are dried out and toasted. This will help give the Kvass its characteristic flavor.

Make the Kvass Base:
- In a large pot, bring the water to a boil. Once boiling, remove the pot from the heat and add the toasted bread cubes to the water.
- Stir the bread cubes into the water, then cover the pot and let it sit at room temperature for 6-8 hours, or overnight. This will allow the bread to infuse the water with its flavor.

Strain the Liquid:
- After the bread has soaked in the water, strain the liquid through a fine-mesh sieve or cheesecloth into a clean container. Press down on the bread cubes to extract as much liquid as possible.

Sweeten and Ferment:
- Stir the sugar into the strained liquid until it dissolves completely. Add the raisins, if using, for extra flavor.
- In a small bowl, dissolve the yeast in a little bit of warm water (about 1/4 cup). Let it sit for 5-10 minutes, or until it becomes frothy.
- Stir the dissolved yeast into the sweetened liquid.

Ferment the Kvass:
- Transfer the sweetened liquid to clean, airtight bottles or jars. Leave some space at the top to allow for fermentation.
- Seal the bottles or jars and let them sit at room temperature for 1-3 days to ferment. During this time, the Kvass will develop its characteristic flavor and carbonation.

- Check the Kvass daily and release any built-up pressure by loosening the lids slightly. Once the Kvass reaches your desired level of fermentation, transfer it to the refrigerator to slow down the fermentation process.

Serve and Enjoy:
- Serve the Kvass chilled, poured into glasses over ice if desired.
- Enjoy this tangy and refreshing fermented drink as a traditional Russian beverage!

Homemade Kvass can be customized with different flavorings such as fruit, herbs, or spices, so feel free to experiment to find your favorite variation. Cheers!

Syrniki (Russian Cottage Cheese Pancakes)

Ingredients:

- 1 cup cottage cheese (drained)
- 1 egg
- 2 tablespoons granulated sugar
- 1/2 teaspoon vanilla extract
- 1/2 cup all-purpose flour
- 1/4 teaspoon baking powder
- Pinch of salt
- Vegetable oil or butter for frying
- Optional toppings: sour cream, jam, honey, fresh berries, powdered sugar

Instructions:

Prepare the Cottage Cheese:
- If the cottage cheese has excess moisture, drain it using a fine-mesh sieve or cheesecloth to remove excess liquid.

Mix the Batter:
- In a mixing bowl, combine the drained cottage cheese, egg, granulated sugar, and vanilla extract. Mix until well combined.

Add Dry Ingredients:
- Sift in the all-purpose flour, baking powder, and a pinch of salt into the bowl with the cottage cheese mixture.

Form the Pancakes:
- Stir the dry ingredients into the cottage cheese mixture until a thick batter forms.
- Heat a skillet or frying pan over medium heat and add a small amount of vegetable oil or butter to grease the surface.
- Scoop about 2 tablespoons of the batter for each pancake and form it into a small disk with your hands. Alternatively, you can use a spoon to shape the batter directly in the skillet.

Cook the Pancakes:
- Place the formed pancakes in the skillet and cook for 2-3 minutes on each side, or until golden brown and cooked through.
- You may need to work in batches depending on the size of your skillet.

Serve:
- Once cooked, transfer the syrniki to a plate lined with paper towels to absorb any excess oil.

- Serve the syrniki warm, topped with your choice of toppings such as sour cream, jam, honey, fresh berries, or powdered sugar.

Enjoy:
- Enjoy these delicious Russian cottage cheese pancakes as a delightful breakfast or dessert treat!

Syrniki are best served warm and fresh, but you can also store any leftovers in an airtight container in the refrigerator for a day or two and reheat them in the microwave or skillet before serving. Enjoy!

Medovik (Russian Honey Cake)

Ingredients:

For the Cake Layers:

- 4 cups all-purpose flour
- 1 teaspoon baking soda
- 1 cup unsalted butter, softened
- 1 cup granulated sugar
- 2 large eggs
- 1 cup honey
- 1/2 cup sour cream

For the Frosting:

- 4 cups sour cream
- 1 cup powdered sugar

Optional Garnish:

- Chopped nuts (such as walnuts or almonds)

Instructions:

For the Cake Layers:

    Prepare the Dough:
- In a large mixing bowl, sift together the flour and baking soda. Set aside.
- In another bowl, cream together the softened butter and granulated sugar until light and fluffy.
- Add the eggs, one at a time, beating well after each addition.
- Stir in the honey and sour cream until well combined.

    Make the Dough:
- Gradually add the sifted flour mixture to the wet ingredients, mixing until a soft dough forms. If the dough is too sticky, add a little more flour as needed.

    Divide and Roll Out:
- Divide the dough into 8 equal portions. Roll out each portion into a thin circle, about 8 inches (20 cm) in diameter.

    Bake the Layers:

- Preheat your oven to 350°F (175°C). Place each rolled-out dough circle on a parchment-lined baking sheet and bake for about 7-8 minutes, or until lightly golden brown.
- Remove from the oven and let the layers cool completely.

For the Frosting:

Prepare the Frosting:
- In a mixing bowl, combine the sour cream and powdered sugar. Mix until smooth and well combined.

Assemble the Medovik:

Layer the Cake:
- Place one baked cake layer on a serving plate or cake stand. Spread a thin layer of frosting evenly over the top.
- Continue layering the remaining cake layers and frosting, ending with a layer of frosting on top. You should have 8 layers of cake and 7 layers of frosting.

Chill the Cake:
- Refrigerate the assembled cake for at least 4 hours, or overnight, to allow the flavors to meld and the frosting to set.

Garnish (Optional):
- Before serving, garnish the top of the cake with chopped nuts, if desired.

Slice and Serve:
- Use a sharp knife to slice the chilled Medovik into portions. Serve and enjoy!

Medovik is a delightful dessert with layers of moist cake and creamy frosting, infused with the rich flavor of honey. It's perfect for special occasions or any time you crave a taste of Russian sweetness. Enjoy!

Okroshka (Cold Summer Soup)

Ingredients:

- 2 medium potatoes, boiled and diced
- 2 medium cucumbers, peeled and diced
- 2 radishes, diced
- 4 hard-boiled eggs, diced
- 1/2 cup fresh dill, chopped
- 1/4 cup fresh parsley, chopped
- 4 cups kefir (Russian fermented milk drink) or kvass (fermented beverage made from rye bread)
- 1 cup water
- 1/2 cup sour cream or Greek yogurt (optional)
- Salt and pepper to taste
- Ice cubes (optional)

Instructions:

Prepare the Ingredients:
- Boil the potatoes until tender, then peel and dice them. Let them cool completely.
- Peel and dice the cucumbers, radishes, and hard-boiled eggs.
- Chop the fresh dill and parsley.

Make the Broth:
- In a large bowl, combine the kefir (or kvass) with water. If using kvass, you may need to dilute it further with additional water, depending on its strength.
- Season the broth with salt and pepper to taste. You can also add a dollop of sour cream or Greek yogurt for extra creaminess if desired.

Assemble the Soup:
- In individual serving bowls, distribute the diced potatoes, cucumbers, radishes, hard-boiled eggs, and chopped herbs evenly.
- Pour the kefir (or kvass) broth over the vegetables in each bowl.

Chill:
- Refrigerate the Okroshka for at least 1-2 hours before serving to allow the flavors to meld and the soup to chill thoroughly.
- You can also add ice cubes to each serving bowl to keep the soup extra cold.

Serve:

- Give the Okroshka a final stir before serving.
- Garnish with additional fresh herbs if desired.
- Serve the cold Okroshka as a refreshing summer soup, accompanied by slices of rye bread or boiled potatoes on the side.

Okroshka is a versatile dish, and you can adjust the ingredients according to your preferences. Some variations include adding diced ham, sausage, or cooked chicken for extra protein. Enjoy this cool and nourishing soup on a hot summer day!

Kartoshka (Russian Chocolate Truffles)

Ingredients:

- 200g (about 7 oz) tea biscuits or digestive biscuits, crushed into fine crumbs
- 1/2 cup cocoa powder (plus extra for coating)
- 1/2 cup sweetened condensed milk
- 1/2 cup unsalted butter, melted
- 1 teaspoon vanilla extract
- Grated chocolate or powdered sugar for coating (optional)

Instructions:

Prepare the Biscuit Crumbs:
- Crush the tea biscuits or digestive biscuits into fine crumbs using a food processor or by placing them in a resealable plastic bag and crushing them with a rolling pin. Transfer the crumbs to a mixing bowl.

Make the Truffle Mixture:
- Add the cocoa powder, sweetened condensed milk, melted butter, and vanilla extract to the bowl with the biscuit crumbs.
- Mix everything together until well combined and a thick, slightly sticky dough forms.

Shape the Truffles:
- Take small portions of the dough and roll them into small balls, about the size of a walnut. The mixture should yield approximately 20-24 truffles.

Coat the Truffles:
- Roll each truffle in cocoa powder until evenly coated. Alternatively, you can roll them in grated chocolate or powdered sugar for a different coating.
- Place the coated truffles on a baking sheet lined with parchment paper.

Chill:
- Transfer the baking sheet with the truffles to the refrigerator and chill for at least 1-2 hours, or until firm.

Serve and Enjoy:
- Once chilled, remove the truffles from the refrigerator and arrange them on a serving platter.
- Serve the Kartoshka truffles as a delightful dessert or snack, and enjoy their rich chocolate flavor and melt-in-your-mouth texture.

Storage:

- Store any leftover truffles in an airtight container in the refrigerator for up to 1 week. Bring them to room temperature before serving for the best taste and texture.

Kartoshka truffles are a beloved treat in Russian cuisine, and they're perfect for satisfying your chocolate cravings without much effort. Enjoy making and indulging in these delicious no-bake delights!

Vatrushka (Russian Sweet Cheese Buns)

Ingredients:

For the Dough:

- 2 1/4 teaspoons (1 packet) active dry yeast
- 1/4 cup warm water (about 110°F/45°C)
- 1/2 cup granulated sugar, divided
- 1/2 cup warm milk (about 110°F/45°C)
- 1/2 cup unsalted butter, melted
- 2 large eggs
- 4 cups all-purpose flour
- 1/2 teaspoon salt

For the Cheese Filling:

- 1 cup farmer's cheese or cottage cheese (drained if necessary)
- 1/4 cup granulated sugar
- 1 egg
- 1 teaspoon vanilla extract
- Optional: raisins or dried fruit for topping

For the Egg Wash:

- 1 egg
- 1 tablespoon water

Instructions:

1. Prepare the Dough:

> In a small bowl, combine the warm water, 1 tablespoon of sugar, and active dry yeast. Let it sit for about 5-10 minutes, or until foamy.
> In a large mixing bowl, combine the warm milk, melted butter, remaining sugar, eggs, and salt. Mix well.
> Add the activated yeast mixture to the bowl and stir to combine.
> Gradually add the flour, mixing until a soft dough forms.
> Knead the dough on a lightly floured surface for about 5-7 minutes, or until smooth and elastic.

Place the dough in a greased bowl, cover with a clean kitchen towel, and let it rise in a warm place for about 1-1.5 hours, or until doubled in size.

2. Make the Cheese Filling:

In a mixing bowl, combine the farmer's cheese (or cottage cheese), granulated sugar, egg, and vanilla extract. Mix until smooth.
Set the filling aside while you prepare the dough.

3. Shape the Vatrushka:

Preheat your oven to 350°F (175°C). Line a baking sheet with parchment paper.
Punch down the risen dough and divide it into equal portions, depending on how large you want your buns.
Roll each portion into a ball and flatten it slightly with your hands to form a disk.
Place the disks on the prepared baking sheet, leaving space between them.
Make an indentation in the center of each disk with your fingers to create a well for the cheese filling.
Fill each indentation with a spoonful of the cheese filling, spreading it out slightly.

4. Bake the Vatrushka:

In a small bowl, whisk together the egg and water to make the egg wash.
Brush the edges of the dough with the egg wash.
If desired, top the cheese filling with raisins or dried fruit.
Bake the vatrushka in the preheated oven for about 20-25 minutes, or until golden brown and the cheese filling is set.
Remove from the oven and let them cool slightly before serving.

5. Serve and Enjoy:

Serve the vatrushka warm or at room temperature.
Enjoy these delicious Russian sweet cheese buns as a delightful breakfast or snack with tea or coffee!

Vatrushka can be stored in an airtight container at room temperature for a day or two, but they are best enjoyed fresh on the day they are made.

Solyanka (Russian Meat and Pickle Soup)

Ingredients:

- 1 lb (450g) mixed meats (such as beef, pork, sausage, ham), diced
- 1 onion, finely chopped
- 2 cloves garlic, minced
- 2 tablespoons vegetable oil
- 4 cups beef or chicken broth
- 1 can (14 oz) diced tomatoes
- 1/4 cup tomato paste
- 1/4 cup pickles, chopped
- 1/4 cup green olives, sliced
- 1/4 cup black olives, sliced
- 2 tablespoons capers
- 1 tablespoon Worcestershire sauce
- 1 tablespoon vinegar (white or apple cider)
- 1 teaspoon paprika
- 1/2 teaspoon dried thyme
- Salt and pepper to taste
- Sour cream, for serving
- Fresh parsley or dill, chopped, for garnish

Instructions:

Sauté the Meats:
- Heat the vegetable oil in a large soup pot over medium heat. Add the diced meats and cook until browned on all sides. Remove the meats from the pot and set aside.

Sauté the Aromatics:
- In the same pot, add the chopped onion and minced garlic. Sauté until softened and fragrant, about 3-4 minutes.

Add Broth and Tomatoes:
- Return the browned meats to the pot. Pour in the beef or chicken broth and add the diced tomatoes (with their juices). Stir to combine.

Add Remaining Ingredients:
- Stir in the tomato paste, chopped pickles, sliced green olives, sliced black olives, capers, Worcestershire sauce, vinegar, paprika, and dried thyme. Season with salt and pepper to taste.

Simmer:

- Bring the soup to a simmer over medium-low heat. Cover and let it simmer for about 30-40 minutes, or until the meats are tender and the flavors have melded together.

Serve:
- Ladle the solyanka into serving bowls. Top each bowl with a dollop of sour cream and a sprinkle of chopped fresh parsley or dill.

Enjoy:
- Serve the solyanka hot, accompanied by crusty bread or Russian rye bread for dipping.

Solyanka is a delicious and satisfying soup that's sure to warm you up on a chilly day. The combination of meats, pickles, and olives gives it a unique and robust flavor that you'll love. Enjoy!

Tvorog (Russian Farmer's Cheese)

Ingredients:

- 1 gallon (about 3.8 liters) whole milk
- 1/4 cup cultured buttermilk or kefir

Instructions:

Heat the Milk:
- Pour the whole milk into a large pot and place it over medium heat. Heat the milk slowly, stirring occasionally, until it reaches a temperature of about 185°F (85°C). Do not let it boil.

Add the Buttermilk or Kefir:
- Once the milk reaches the desired temperature, remove it from the heat.
- Stir in the cultured buttermilk or kefir, using a whisk or spoon to mix it thoroughly with the milk.

Allow to Curdle:
- Cover the pot with a clean kitchen towel or lid and let it sit at room temperature for 12-24 hours. During this time, the milk will curdle and form curds.

Strain the Curds:
- Line a large colander or sieve with cheesecloth and place it over a bowl or in the sink.
- Carefully pour the curdled milk mixture into the cheesecloth-lined colander, allowing the whey (liquid) to drain away.
- Let the curds drain for several hours, or until they reach the desired consistency. The longer you let them drain, the firmer the Tvorog will be.

Press the Cheese (Optional):
- If you prefer a firmer texture, you can place a weight on top of the cheesecloth-wrapped curds to press out more whey. This will result in a denser cheese.

Store or Use:
- Once the whey has drained away and you're happy with the texture of the Tvorog, transfer it to a clean container and refrigerate it until ready to use.
- Tvorog can be stored in the refrigerator for up to a week.

Enjoy:
- Use your homemade Tvorog as a spread on bread or toast, mix it into pancakes or blini batter, or use it as a filling for pierogi, blintzes, or cakes.

It's also delicious when sweetened with honey or sugar and topped with fruit or jam.

Making Tvorog at home is a simple process that allows you to enjoy this versatile cheese in a variety of dishes. Experiment with different flavors and uses to discover your favorite way to enjoy Tvorog!

Sirniki (Russian Farmer's Cheese Pancakes)

Ingredients:

- 2 cups tvorog (Russian farmer's cheese or cottage cheese), well-drained
- 1/4 cup granulated sugar
- 2 large eggs
- 1/2 teaspoon vanilla extract
- 1/2 cup all-purpose flour (plus extra for dusting)
- 1/4 teaspoon baking powder
- Pinch of salt
- Vegetable oil or butter, for frying
- Sour cream, jam, honey, or fresh berries, for serving

Instructions:

Prepare the Tvorog:
- If your tvorog or cottage cheese is wet, drain it using a fine-mesh sieve or cheesecloth to remove excess moisture. You want the cheese to be as dry as possible.

Mix the Batter:
- In a large mixing bowl, combine the well-drained tvorog, granulated sugar, eggs, and vanilla extract. Mix until well combined.

Add Dry Ingredients:
- Sift in the all-purpose flour, baking powder, and a pinch of salt into the bowl with the cheese mixture. Mix until smooth and well combined. The batter should be thick and slightly sticky.

Shape the Pancakes:
- Lightly dust your hands with flour to prevent sticking. Take small portions of the batter and shape them into small patties or disks, about 2-3 inches (5-7 cm) in diameter and 1/2 inch (1 cm) thick. You should get about 8-10 pancakes depending on the size.

Fry the Sirniki:
- Heat a skillet or frying pan over medium heat and add a small amount of vegetable oil or butter to grease the surface.
- Carefully place the shaped pancakes in the skillet, making sure not to overcrowd the pan. Cook for 2-3 minutes on each side, or until golden brown and cooked through.

Serve:

- Serve the sirniki hot, garnished with a dollop of sour cream and a spoonful of jam, honey, or fresh berries on top.
- Enjoy these delicious Russian farmer's cheese pancakes for breakfast, dessert, or as a sweet snack!

Sirniki are best enjoyed fresh and warm, but you can also store any leftovers in an airtight container in the refrigerator for a day or two and reheat them in the microwave or skillet before serving. Experiment with different toppings and flavors to create your favorite variation of sirniki!

Zapekanka (Russian Baked Cheesecake)

Ingredients:

- 500g tvorog (Russian farmer's cheese or cottage cheese), drained
- 3 large eggs
- 1/2 cup granulated sugar
- 1/2 cup sour cream
- 1 teaspoon vanilla extract
- 2 tablespoons semolina or flour
- Zest of 1 lemon (optional)
- Butter or oil, for greasing the baking dish
- Powdered sugar, for dusting (optional)
- Fresh berries or fruit compote, for serving (optional)

Instructions:

Preheat the Oven:
- Preheat your oven to 350°F (175°C). Grease a baking dish with butter or oil.

Prepare the Tvorog:
- If your tvorog or cottage cheese is very wet, drain it in a fine-mesh sieve or cheesecloth-lined colander for about 30 minutes to remove excess moisture.

Mix the Batter:
- In a large mixing bowl, combine the drained tvorog, eggs, granulated sugar, sour cream, vanilla extract, semolina or flour, and lemon zest (if using). Mix until smooth and well combined.

Bake the Zapekanka:
- Pour the batter into the greased baking dish, spreading it out evenly.
- Bake in the preheated oven for 40-50 minutes, or until the top is golden brown and the center is set. The exact baking time may vary depending on your oven and the size of your baking dish.

Cool and Serve:
- Remove the zapekanka from the oven and let it cool slightly before serving.
- Dust with powdered sugar if desired, and serve slices of zapekanka warm or at room temperature.
- Enjoy your delicious Russian baked cheesecake on its own or with fresh berries or fruit compote on the side.

Zapekanka is a delightful dessert that's perfect for any occasion, whether you're hosting a gathering or simply craving a sweet treat. Its creamy texture and subtle sweetness make it a favorite among both kids and adults. Enjoy!

Zavtrak (Russian Breakfast Pancakes)

Ingredients:

- 1 cup all-purpose flour
- 1 tablespoon granulated sugar (optional)
- 1 teaspoon baking powder
- 1/4 teaspoon salt
- 1 cup milk
- 1 large egg
- 2 tablespoons unsalted butter, melted
- Butter or oil, for cooking
- Sour cream, jam, honey, or fresh fruit, for serving (optional)

Instructions:

Prepare the Batter:
- In a mixing bowl, whisk together the flour, sugar (if using), baking powder, and salt until well combined.

Add Wet Ingredients:
- In another bowl, whisk together the milk, egg, and melted butter until smooth.

Combine Wet and Dry Ingredients:
- Pour the wet ingredients into the dry ingredients and stir until just combined. Be careful not to overmix; it's okay if the batter is slightly lumpy.

Let the Batter Rest:
- Let the batter rest for about 10-15 minutes. This allows the baking powder to activate and helps ensure fluffy pancakes.

Cook the Pancakes:
- Heat a skillet or griddle over medium heat and grease it with butter or oil.
- Pour about 1/4 cup of batter onto the skillet for each pancake. Cook until bubbles form on the surface of the pancake and the edges look set, about 2-3 minutes.

Flip and Cook the Other Side:
- Carefully flip the pancakes using a spatula and cook for an additional 1-2 minutes, or until golden brown on the bottom and cooked through.

Serve:
- Serve the pancakes warm, with your choice of toppings such as sour cream, jam, honey, or fresh fruit.

Russian breakfast pancakes are a delicious and versatile option for starting your day.

Whether you prefer them sweet or savory, they're sure to be a hit at the breakfast table!

Kasha (Russian Porridge)

Ingredients:

- 1 cup buckwheat groats
- 2 cups water or broth
- 1 tablespoon butter or vegetable oil
- Salt, to taste

Instructions:

Rinse the Buckwheat Groats:
- Place the buckwheat groats in a fine-mesh sieve and rinse them under cold water until the water runs clear. This helps remove any debris and excess starch from the groats.

Toast the Buckwheat Groats (Optional):
- In a dry skillet over medium heat, toast the rinsed buckwheat groats for 3-4 minutes, stirring occasionally, until they are lightly golden and fragrant. This step is optional but can enhance the nutty flavor of the kasha.

Cook the Buckwheat Kasha:
- In a saucepan, bring the water or broth to a boil over high heat.
- Once boiling, add the toasted buckwheat groats to the saucepan.
- Reduce the heat to low, cover the saucepan with a lid, and simmer for about 15-20 minutes, or until the buckwheat is tender and has absorbed most of the liquid. Stir occasionally to prevent sticking.

Fluff and Season:
- Once the buckwheat is cooked, remove the saucepan from the heat.
- Stir in the butter or vegetable oil until melted and well incorporated.
- Season the kasha with salt to taste, adjusting as needed.

Serve:
- Serve the buckwheat kasha hot as a breakfast porridge or as a side dish with savory toppings such as sautéed mushrooms, caramelized onions, or cooked vegetables.
- You can also enjoy buckwheat kasha with a drizzle of honey or maple syrup for a sweeter variation.

Buckwheat kasha is nutritious, hearty, and versatile, making it a popular choice for a comforting meal any time of day. Experiment with different grains and toppings to create your favorite version of Russian kasha!

Guriev Kasha (Russian Buckwheat Porridge)

Ingredients:

- 1 cup buckwheat groats
- 2 cups water or broth
- 2 tablespoons butter or vegetable oil
- Salt to taste
- Optional: chopped onions or garlic for flavor

Instructions:

Rinse the buckwheat groats under cold water until the water runs clear. This helps remove any excess starch and bitterness.
In a saucepan, melt the butter or heat the vegetable oil over medium heat.
If using onions or garlic, sauté them in the butter or oil until they are soft and fragrant.
Add the rinsed buckwheat groats to the saucepan and toast them, stirring frequently, for about 3-4 minutes. This step helps enhance the nutty flavor of the buckwheat.
Pour in the water or broth and add salt to taste. Bring the mixture to a boil.
Once boiling, reduce the heat to low, cover the saucepan with a lid, and simmer for about 15-20 minutes, or until the buckwheat is tender and has absorbed most of the liquid. Keep an eye on it and stir occasionally to prevent sticking.
Once the buckwheat is cooked, remove the saucepan from the heat and let it sit, covered, for a few minutes to allow any remaining liquid to be absorbed.
Fluff the Guriev Kasha with a fork and serve hot as a side dish or topped with your favorite garnishes, such as fresh herbs or sour cream.

Guriev Kasha is a versatile dish that can be enjoyed on its own or paired with meats, vegetables, or sauces according to personal preference. It's nutritious, hearty, and perfect for a comforting meal, particularly during colder months.

Russian Meatballs in Tomato Sauce

Ingredients:

For the Meatballs:

- 500g ground beef (or a mix of beef and pork)
- 1 small onion, finely chopped
- 2 cloves garlic, minced
- 1/3 cup breadcrumbs
- 1 egg
- 2 tablespoons milk
- 1 teaspoon salt
- 1/2 teaspoon black pepper
- 1/2 teaspoon paprika (optional)
- 1/4 cup fresh parsley, chopped (optional)

For the Tomato Sauce:

- 2 tablespoons olive oil
- 1 onion, finely chopped
- 2 cloves garlic, minced
- 1 can (400g) diced tomatoes
- 1 tablespoon tomato paste
- 1 teaspoon sugar
- 1 teaspoon salt
- 1/2 teaspoon black pepper
- 1 teaspoon dried herbs (such as oregano, thyme, or basil)
- 1 bay leaf

Instructions:

1. Prepare the Meatballs:

   In a large bowl, combine the ground meat, chopped onion, minced garlic, breadcrumbs, egg, milk, salt, pepper, paprika, and chopped parsley (if using).

Mix everything together until well combined. Avoid overmixing to keep the meatballs tender.

Shape the mixture into meatballs, about the size of golf balls, and place them on a plate or tray. You should get around 20 meatballs.

2. Cook the Meatballs:

Heat olive oil in a large skillet or frying pan over medium heat.
Add the meatballs to the skillet in batches, making sure not to overcrowd the pan. Cook them for about 3-4 minutes per side, or until browned and cooked through.
Transfer the cooked meatballs to a plate and set aside.

3. Prepare the Tomato Sauce:

In the same skillet, add a bit more olive oil if needed. Sauté the chopped onion and minced garlic until softened and fragrant, about 3-4 minutes.
Add the diced tomatoes (with their juices), tomato paste, sugar, salt, pepper, dried herbs, and bay leaf to the skillet. Stir to combine.
Bring the sauce to a simmer and let it cook for about 10 minutes, stirring occasionally, to allow the flavors to meld together and the sauce to thicken slightly.

4. Combine and Simmer:

Return the cooked meatballs to the skillet with the tomato sauce. Spoon some of the sauce over the meatballs to coat them evenly.
Cover the skillet and let the meatballs simmer in the sauce for an additional 10-15 minutes, allowing the flavors to blend further.

5. Serve:

Once the meatballs are heated through and the sauce has thickened to your liking, remove the skillet from the heat.
Serve the Russian meatballs in tomato sauce hot, garnished with fresh parsley or dill if desired. They can be served as a main dish with a side of mashed potatoes, rice, or pasta, or as an appetizer with crusty bread for dipping into the sauce.

Enjoy your delicious Russian meatballs in tomato sauce!

Russian Black Bread (Pumpernickel)

Ingredients:

- 2 cups rye flour
- 2 cups bread flour (or all-purpose flour)
- 1 cup whole wheat flour
- 1 1/2 cups lukewarm water
- 2 tablespoons molasses or dark corn syrup
- 2 tablespoons unsweetened cocoa powder
- 2 tablespoons caraway seeds (optional)
- 2 teaspoons instant yeast
- 1 1/2 teaspoons salt
- 1 tablespoon vegetable oil or melted butter, for greasing

Instructions:

Activate the Yeast: In a small bowl, combine the lukewarm water and molasses. Sprinkle the instant yeast over the mixture and let it sit for about 5-10 minutes, or until foamy.

Mix the Dough: In a large mixing bowl, combine the rye flour, bread flour, whole wheat flour, cocoa powder, caraway seeds (if using), and salt. Mix well to combine.

Make a well in the center of the dry ingredients and pour in the activated yeast mixture. Stir until a rough dough forms.

Knead the Dough: Turn the dough out onto a lightly floured surface and knead it for about 8-10 minutes, or until it becomes smooth and elastic. Add more flour as needed to prevent sticking, but keep in mind that the dough will be slightly sticky due to the high proportion of rye flour.

First Rise: Place the kneaded dough in a lightly greased bowl, turning once to coat the dough with oil. Cover the bowl with a clean kitchen towel or plastic wrap and let the dough rise in a warm, draft-free place for about 1-1.5 hours, or until doubled in size.

Shape the Loaf: Once the dough has risen, punch it down to release the air. Shape it into a round or oval loaf and place it on a parchment-lined baking sheet. You can also place the loaf in a greased loaf pan if you prefer a more structured shape.

Second Rise: Cover the shaped loaf with a clean kitchen towel and let it rise for another 30-45 minutes, or until slightly puffed.

Preheat the Oven: While the dough is rising, preheat your oven to 375°F (190°C).
Bake the Bread: Once the dough has finished its second rise, slash the top of the loaf with a sharp knife to allow for expansion during baking. Bake in the preheated oven for 35-45 minutes, or until the bread is dark golden brown and sounds hollow when tapped on the bottom.
Cool and Serve: Remove the bread from the oven and transfer it to a wire rack to cool completely before slicing. Russian black bread is best served slightly warm or at room temperature, and it pairs well with butter, cheese, smoked fish, or hearty soups and stews.

Enjoy your homemade Russian black bread!

Russian Tea Samovar

Ingredients:

- Black tea leaves or tea bags
- Water
- Lemon slices
- Sugar, honey, or sweeteners (optional)
- Jam or preserves (optional, for serving)

Equipment:

- Samovar
- Teapot
- Teacups
- Tea strainer (if using loose tea leaves)

Instructions:

Prepare the Samovar:
- Place the samovar on a stable surface.
- Fill the body of the samovar with water, leaving some space at the top to prevent spillage when heating.
- Open the fuel compartment and add charcoal, wood, or other fuel according to the manufacturer's instructions.
- Light the fuel and allow the water to heat up. Traditional samovars were kept burning continuously to keep the water hot throughout the day.

Prepare the Tea:
- Meanwhile, prepare your tea in a separate teapot. Use black tea leaves or tea bags, depending on your preference.
- If using loose tea leaves, place them in the teapot and pour hot water over them. Let the tea steep for 3-5 minutes, or according to your preference.
- If using tea bags, simply place them in the teapot and pour hot water over them. Let them steep for a few minutes.

Serve the Tea:
- Once the water in the samovar is hot, place the teapot on top of the samovar to keep the tea warm.

- Arrange lemon slices, sugar, honey, or sweeteners on the table for guests to add to their tea as desired.
- Guests can fill their teacups with hot water from the samovar and then add tea from the teapot. Use a tea strainer if using loose tea leaves to catch any sediment.

Enjoy:
- Russian tea drinking is a social affair, often accompanied by conversation, snacks, or sweets such as jam or preserves.
- Sip your tea slowly and enjoy the warmth and camaraderie of the gathering.

Maintaining the Samovar:
- Keep an eye on the fuel level in the samovar and add more fuel as needed to keep the water hot.
- Periodically clean the samovar according to the manufacturer's instructions to remove any buildup or residue.

With this recipe and method, you can enjoy the tradition of Russian tea served from a classic samovar, bringing warmth and hospitality to any gathering.

Rassolnik (Russian Pickle Soup)

Ingredients:

- 1 cup pearl barley
- 1 onion, finely chopped
- 2 carrots, peeled and diced
- 2 celery stalks, diced
- 2 tablespoons vegetable oil
- 500g beef or veal, diced (you can also use chicken or pork)
- 6 cups beef or vegetable broth
- 1 cup dill pickles, chopped
- 1/2 cup pickle brine (liquid from the pickle jar)
- 2 bay leaves
- 4-5 whole black peppercorns
- Salt and pepper, to taste
- Sour cream, for serving (optional)
- Fresh dill or parsley, chopped, for garnish

Instructions:

Prepare the Barley: Rinse the pearl barley under cold water. In a medium saucepan, bring 4 cups of water to a boil. Add the rinsed barley and cook according to package instructions until tender, about 25-30 minutes. Drain and set aside.

Sauté the Vegetables: In a large pot or Dutch oven, heat the vegetable oil over medium heat. Add the chopped onion, diced carrots, and diced celery. Sauté until the vegetables are softened, about 5-7 minutes.

Brown the Meat: Push the sautéed vegetables to the side of the pot and add the diced beef or veal to the center. Brown the meat on all sides, about 5 minutes.

Add Broth and Seasonings: Pour in the beef or vegetable broth, scraping the bottom of the pot to loosen any browned bits. Add the cooked barley, chopped dill pickles, pickle brine, bay leaves, and whole black peppercorns. Season with salt and pepper to taste.

Simmer the Soup: Bring the soup to a simmer over medium-low heat. Cover the pot and let the soup simmer gently for about 30-40 minutes, or until the meat is tender and the flavors have melded together.

Adjust Seasonings: Taste the soup and adjust the seasoning with more salt and pepper if needed. You can also add more pickle brine for extra tanginess, if desired.

Serve: Ladle the hot Rassolnik into bowls. Garnish each serving with a dollop of sour cream (if using) and a sprinkle of fresh dill or parsley.

Enjoy: Serve the Rassolnik hot as a comforting and satisfying meal. It pairs well with crusty bread or toasted rye bread on the side.

This recipe makes a delicious and warming Rassolnik soup that's sure to be a hit with family and friends. Enjoy!

Kompot (Russian Fruit Punch)

Ingredients:

- 4-5 cups mixed fruits (such as apples, pears, berries, peaches, apricots, cherries, or plums), washed and chopped
- 6-8 cups water
- 1/2 to 3/4 cup sugar (adjust according to taste and sweetness of fruits)
- 1 cinnamon stick (optional)
- 3-4 cloves (optional)
- Lemon slices or juice (optional, for extra flavor)

Instructions:

Prepare the Fruits: Wash the fruits thoroughly and chop them into bite-sized pieces. You can leave the skins on for added flavor and color, or peel them if desired.

Combine Ingredients in a Pot: In a large pot, combine the chopped fruits, water, sugar, and any optional spices (such as cinnamon stick and cloves). If using lemon, you can add slices directly to the pot or squeeze lemon juice into the mixture.

Simmer the Kompot: Place the pot over medium heat and bring the mixture to a gentle boil. Once boiling, reduce the heat to low and let the Kompot simmer uncovered for about 20-30 minutes, or until the fruits are soft and the flavors have infused the liquid.

Adjust Sweetness: Taste the Kompot and adjust the sweetness by adding more sugar if necessary. Keep in mind that the sweetness will depend on the natural sugars in the fruits used.

Cool and Strain (Optional): Once the Kompot is done simmering, remove it from the heat and let it cool slightly. If you prefer a clear Kompot without fruit pieces, you can strain the mixture through a fine-mesh sieve or cheesecloth to remove the fruit solids. Alternatively, you can leave the fruit pieces in for added texture.

Serve: Serve the Kompot hot or cold, depending on your preference and the season. If serving cold, refrigerate the Kompot until chilled. You can also serve it with ice cubes for extra refreshment.

Garnish (Optional): Garnish individual servings of Kompot with fresh mint leaves or additional fruit slices for a decorative touch.

Enjoy: Kompot is a delightful and versatile beverage that can be enjoyed on its own or as a complement to meals. It's perfect for special occasions, gatherings, or simply as a refreshing drink on a hot day.

This recipe yields a delicious and customizable Kompot that showcases the natural sweetness and flavors of seasonal fruits. Feel free to experiment with different fruit combinations and adjust the sweetness to suit your taste preferences.

Russian Beef and Mushroom Stew

Ingredients:

- 500g beef stew meat, cut into cubes
- 2 tablespoons vegetable oil
- 1 onion, finely chopped
- 2 cloves garlic, minced
- 200g mushrooms, sliced (such as button mushrooms or cremini)
- 2 carrots, peeled and diced
- 2 potatoes, peeled and diced
- 2 cups beef broth
- 1 cup water
- 2 tablespoons tomato paste
- 1 teaspoon paprika
- 1 teaspoon dried thyme
- Salt and pepper, to taste
- Chopped fresh parsley, for garnish

Instructions:

Brown the Beef: Heat the vegetable oil in a large pot or Dutch oven over medium-high heat. Add the beef cubes in batches and brown them on all sides. Remove the beef from the pot and set aside.

Sauté the Vegetables: In the same pot, add the chopped onion and minced garlic. Sauté until the onion is translucent and fragrant, about 3-4 minutes. Add the sliced mushrooms and diced carrots to the pot and cook for another 5 minutes, or until the mushrooms are tender.

Add the Remaining Ingredients: Return the browned beef to the pot. Add the diced potatoes, beef broth, water, tomato paste, paprika, and dried thyme. Stir to combine all the ingredients.

Simmer the Stew: Bring the stew to a boil, then reduce the heat to low. Cover the pot and let the stew simmer gently for about 1.5 to 2 hours, or until the beef is tender and the flavors have melded together. Stir occasionally and check the liquid level, adding more water or broth if needed.

Season and Serve: Once the stew is done cooking, season with salt and pepper to taste. Garnish with chopped fresh parsley before serving.

Serve: Ladle the beef and mushroom stew into bowls and serve hot. You can enjoy it on its own or with a side of crusty bread, rice, or mashed potatoes for a complete and satisfying meal.

Store: Leftovers can be stored in an airtight container in the refrigerator for up to 3 days or frozen for longer storage. Reheat gently on the stove or in the microwave before serving.

This Russian beef and mushroom stew is a comforting and flavorful dish that's perfect for chilly days. The combination of tender beef, savory mushrooms, and hearty vegetables creates a satisfying meal that the whole family will love.

Pryanik (Russian Honey-Spice Cake)

Ingredients:

- 2 cups all-purpose flour
- 1 teaspoon baking soda
- 1 teaspoon ground cinnamon
- 1/2 teaspoon ground ginger
- 1/4 teaspoon ground cloves
- 1/4 teaspoon ground nutmeg
- 1/4 teaspoon salt
- 1/2 cup unsalted butter, softened
- 1/2 cup granulated sugar
- 1/2 cup honey
- 1 large egg
- 1/4 cup sour cream or plain yogurt
- Optional: chopped nuts, dried fruits, or candied citrus peel for extra flavor and texture

For the Glaze (optional):

- 1 cup powdered sugar
- 1-2 tablespoons milk or water
- 1/2 teaspoon vanilla extract

Instructions:

Preheat the Oven: Preheat your oven to 350°F (175°C). Grease and flour a baking pan or line it with parchment paper for easy removal.
Prepare the Dry Ingredients: In a medium bowl, sift together the all-purpose flour, baking soda, ground cinnamon, ground ginger, ground cloves, ground nutmeg, and salt. Set aside.
Cream the Butter and Sugar: In a large mixing bowl, cream together the softened butter and granulated sugar until light and fluffy.
Add the Wet Ingredients: Beat in the honey, egg, and sour cream (or plain yogurt) until well combined.

Combine the Batter: Gradually add the dry ingredients to the wet ingredients, mixing until a smooth batter forms. If using, fold in the chopped nuts, dried fruits, or candied citrus peel at this stage.

Bake the Cake: Pour the batter into the prepared baking pan and spread it evenly. Bake in the preheated oven for 25-30 minutes, or until a toothpick inserted into the center comes out clean.

Cool the Cake: Allow the cake to cool in the pan for 10 minutes, then transfer it to a wire rack to cool completely.

Prepare the Glaze (optional): In a small bowl, whisk together the powdered sugar, milk or water, and vanilla extract until smooth. Adjust the consistency by adding more liquid if too thick or more powdered sugar if too thin.

Glaze the Cake (optional): Once the cake has cooled, drizzle the glaze over the top using a spoon or spatula. Allow the glaze to set before slicing and serving the cake.

Serve: Slice the Pryanik into squares or rectangles and serve it as a delicious dessert or snack with tea or coffee.

This homemade Pryanik recipe captures the essence of traditional Russian honey-spice cake, making it perfect for special occasions or simply as a treat for yourself and your loved ones. Enjoy the warm flavors of honey and spices in every bite!

Russkaya Salat (Russian Salad)

Ingredients:

- 3 medium potatoes, peeled and diced
- 2 carrots, peeled and diced
- 1 cup frozen peas, thawed
- 4 hard-boiled eggs, diced
- 3-4 pickles, diced
- 1/2 cup diced cooked ham or chicken (optional)
- 1/2 cup diced cooked sausage (optional)
- 1/2 cup mayonnaise
- 2 tablespoons sour cream or plain yogurt
- 1 tablespoon Dijon mustard (optional)
- Salt and pepper, to taste
- Fresh dill or parsley, chopped, for garnish (optional)

Instructions:

Prepare the Vegetables: In a large pot, bring salted water to a boil. Add the diced potatoes and carrots and cook until tender, about 10-15 minutes. Drain and let them cool completely.

Assemble the Salad: In a large mixing bowl, combine the cooked potatoes, carrots, thawed peas, diced hard-boiled eggs, diced pickles, and any optional ingredients such as cooked ham or sausage.

Make the Dressing: In a small bowl, whisk together the mayonnaise, sour cream or plain yogurt, and Dijon mustard (if using). Season with salt and pepper to taste.

Dress the Salad: Pour the dressing over the salad ingredients in the mixing bowl. Gently toss until everything is evenly coated with the dressing.

Chill: Cover the bowl with plastic wrap or transfer the salad to an airtight container. Refrigerate for at least 1-2 hours to allow the flavors to meld together and the salad to chill.

Serve: Before serving, give the salad a final toss to redistribute the dressing. Garnish with chopped fresh dill or parsley, if desired.

Enjoy: Russkaya Salat is typically served as a side dish or appetizer, but it can also be enjoyed as a light meal on its own. Serve chilled and enjoy the delicious flavors of this classic Russian salad.

This recipe is versatile, and you can adjust the ingredients according to your preferences. Some variations of Russkaya Salat may include additional ingredients such as diced apples, cooked beets, or canned corn. Feel free to customize the salad to suit your taste!

Russkaya Ribka (Russian Fish Pie)

Ingredients:

For the Pastry:

- 2 sheets of puff pastry, thawed if frozen

For the Filling:

- 500g white fish fillets (such as cod, haddock, or tilapia), cut into bite-sized pieces
- 1 onion, finely chopped
- 2 carrots, peeled and diced
- 1 celery stalk, diced
- 2 tablespoons butter or oil
- 2 tablespoons all-purpose flour
- 1 cup fish or vegetable broth
- 1/2 cup heavy cream or sour cream
- 1 tablespoon lemon juice
- Salt and pepper, to taste
- Chopped fresh dill or parsley, for garnish

For Egg Wash (optional):

- 1 egg, beaten

Instructions:

Preheat the Oven: Preheat your oven to 375°F (190°C). Line a baking sheet with parchment paper.
Prepare the Filling:
- In a large skillet, melt the butter over medium heat. Add the chopped onion, diced carrots, and diced celery. Sauté until the vegetables are softened, about 5-7 minutes.
- Stir in the all-purpose flour and cook for another 1-2 minutes to make a roux.

- Gradually pour in the fish or vegetable broth, stirring constantly to prevent lumps from forming.
- Stir in the heavy cream or sour cream and lemon juice. Cook for a few minutes until the sauce thickens slightly.
- Season the sauce with salt and pepper to taste. Remove the skillet from the heat and let the sauce cool slightly.

Assemble the Pie:

- Place one sheet of puff pastry on the prepared baking sheet. Spread the cooled sauce evenly over the pastry, leaving a border around the edges.
- Arrange the fish pieces on top of the sauce.
- Place the second sheet of puff pastry over the filling. Press the edges of the pastry sheets together to seal, and crimp the edges with a fork to create a decorative border.
- If desired, brush the top of the pie with beaten egg to create a golden crust.

Bake the Pie:

- Transfer the assembled pie to the preheated oven and bake for 25-30 minutes, or until the pastry is puffed and golden brown, and the filling is heated through and bubbly.

Serve:

- Remove the Russkaya Ribka from the oven and let it cool slightly before slicing.
- Garnish with chopped fresh dill or parsley before serving.

Enjoy:

- Russkaya Ribka is best served warm as a comforting main dish. It pairs well with a side salad or steamed vegetables.

This recipe yields a delicious Russkaya Ribka with a creamy and flavorful filling encased in flaky puff pastry. Feel free to customize the filling with your favorite fish and vegetables, and adjust the seasonings to suit your taste preferences.

Russian Mushroom and Potato Soup

Ingredients:

- 2 tablespoons butter or vegetable oil
- 1 onion, finely chopped
- 2 cloves garlic, minced
- 500g mushrooms, sliced (any variety you prefer)
- 3 medium potatoes, peeled and diced
- 4 cups vegetable or chicken broth
- 1 cup milk or heavy cream
- 1 bay leaf
- 1 teaspoon dried thyme (or use fresh thyme sprigs)
- Salt and pepper, to taste
- Chopped fresh parsley or dill, for garnish

Instructions:

Sauté the Vegetables: In a large pot or Dutch oven, melt the butter or heat the vegetable oil over medium heat. Add the chopped onion and minced garlic, and sauté until softened and fragrant, about 3-4 minutes.

Add the Mushrooms: Add the sliced mushrooms to the pot and cook until they release their juices and start to brown, about 5-7 minutes.

Add Potatoes and Broth: Add the diced potatoes to the pot, followed by the vegetable or chicken broth. Stir to combine.

Simmer the Soup: Bring the soup to a simmer over medium heat. Add the bay leaf and dried thyme (or fresh thyme sprigs), then reduce the heat to low. Cover the pot and let the soup simmer gently for about 15-20 minutes, or until the potatoes are tender.

Blend (Optional): If you prefer a smoother consistency, you can use an immersion blender to blend part of the soup until smooth. Alternatively, you can transfer a portion of the soup to a blender and blend until smooth, then return it to the pot.

Add Milk or Cream: Stir in the milk or heavy cream to the soup, and let it simmer for another 5 minutes. This will add creaminess to the soup.

Season and Serve: Season the soup with salt and pepper to taste. Remove the bay leaf and thyme sprigs, if using. Ladle the soup into bowls and garnish with chopped fresh parsley or dill.

Enjoy: Serve the Russian Mushroom and Potato Soup hot, accompanied by crusty bread or crackers for dipping. It makes for a comforting and satisfying meal, especially during colder months.

Feel free to customize this soup by adding other vegetables such as carrots or celery, or by using different types of mushrooms for added flavor. Adjust the thickness of the soup by adding more broth or cream according to your preference.

Russian Eggplant Caviar (Ikra)

Ingredients:

- 2 large eggplants
- 2 tomatoes, diced
- 1 onion, finely chopped
- 2 cloves garlic, minced
- 2 tablespoons vegetable oil
- 1 tablespoon tomato paste
- 1 tablespoon red wine vinegar or lemon juice
- Salt and pepper, to taste
- Fresh herbs (such as parsley or dill), chopped, for garnish (optional)

Instructions:

Roast the Eggplants:
- Preheat your oven to 400°F (200°C). Line a baking sheet with parchment paper.
- Pierce the eggplants with a fork in several places to prevent them from bursting while roasting. Place them on the prepared baking sheet.
- Roast the eggplants in the preheated oven for 40-50 minutes, or until they are tender and collapsed. Remove from the oven and let them cool slightly.

Prepare the Eggplant Flesh:
- Once the eggplants are cool enough to handle, cut them in half lengthwise. Scoop out the flesh from the skins and transfer it to a bowl. Discard the skins.

Cook the Vegetables:
- In a large skillet or frying pan, heat the vegetable oil over medium heat. Add the finely chopped onion and minced garlic, and sauté until softened and fragrant, about 3-4 minutes.
- Add the diced tomatoes to the skillet and cook for another 5 minutes, or until they start to break down and release their juices.

Combine Ingredients:
- Add the roasted eggplant flesh to the skillet with the cooked onions, garlic, and tomatoes. Stir in the tomato paste and red wine vinegar or lemon juice. Mix well to combine all the ingredients.

Simmer the Mixture:

- Reduce the heat to low and let the mixture simmer gently for about 10-15 minutes, stirring occasionally, to allow the flavors to meld together and the mixture to thicken slightly.

Season and Serve:
- Season the eggplant caviar with salt and pepper to taste. If desired, stir in chopped fresh herbs such as parsley or dill for added flavor and freshness.
- Remove the skillet from the heat and let the eggplant caviar cool slightly before serving.

Enjoy:
- Serve the Russian Eggplant Caviar warm or at room temperature as a spread on bread or crackers, or as a side dish to accompany a meal. It's also delicious as a topping for grilled meats or fish.

This homemade Russian Eggplant Caviar is flavorful, creamy, and perfect for sharing with friends and family. Enjoy its rich taste and versatility as a delicious addition to your table!

Russian Pickled Vegetables (Selyoniy)

Ingredients:

- 2 large cucumbers, sliced
- 2 carrots, peeled and thinly sliced
- 1 bell pepper, sliced
- 1 small cabbage, thinly sliced
- 1 onion, thinly sliced
- 4 cloves garlic, minced
- 2-3 bay leaves
- 1 tablespoon whole black peppercorns
- 1 tablespoon mustard seeds
- 1 tablespoon coriander seeds
- 1 tablespoon dill seeds (or use fresh dill)
- 1 teaspoon red pepper flakes (optional, for extra heat)
- 4 cups water
- 1 cup white vinegar
- 2 tablespoons salt
- 2 tablespoons sugar

Instructions:

Prepare the Vegetables:
- Wash and prepare the vegetables by slicing them into thin rounds or strips. You can also use a mandoline slicer for uniform slices.

Make the Brine:
- In a large pot, combine the water, white vinegar, salt, and sugar. Stir until the salt and sugar are dissolved.
- Add the minced garlic, bay leaves, black peppercorns, mustard seeds, coriander seeds, dill seeds, and red pepper flakes (if using) to the pot. Stir to combine.

Bring to a Boil:
- Bring the brine mixture to a boil over medium-high heat. Let it boil for 1-2 minutes to allow the flavors to meld together.

Pack the Vegetables:
- Meanwhile, pack the prepared vegetables tightly into clean, sterilized jars. You can layer the different vegetables or mix them together in each jar.

Pour the Brine:
- Carefully pour the hot brine over the vegetables in the jars, covering them completely. Leave about 1/2 inch of space at the top of each jar.

Seal the Jars:
- Wipe the rims of the jars with a clean, damp cloth to remove any brine or residue. Place the lids on the jars and screw them on tightly.

Cool and Refrigerate:
- Let the jars cool to room temperature on the counter. Once cooled, refrigerate the pickled vegetables for at least 24 hours before serving to allow the flavors to develop.

Serve:
- Russian pickled vegetables can be served cold as a side dish or snack. They pair well with sandwiches, salads, or as an accompaniment to grilled meats or fish.

Storage:
- Store the pickled vegetables in the refrigerator for up to several weeks. The flavors will continue to develop over time, making them even more delicious.

Enjoy your homemade Russian pickled vegetables as a tasty and tangy addition to your meals or as a delightful snack! Adjust the spices and seasonings according to your taste preferences for a personalized flavor profile.

Russian Beet Salad (Vinegret)

Ingredients:

- 2 medium beets, cooked, peeled, and diced
- 2 medium potatoes, cooked, peeled, and diced
- 2 medium carrots, cooked, peeled, and diced
- 1 onion, finely chopped
- 1 large dill pickle, diced
- 1 cup canned or cooked green peas
- 2-3 tablespoons vegetable oil (such as sunflower oil)
- 2 tablespoons apple cider vinegar or white wine vinegar
- 1 teaspoon Dijon mustard
- Salt and pepper, to taste
- Chopped fresh dill or parsley, for garnish (optional)

Instructions:

Prepare the Vegetables:
- Cook the beets, potatoes, and carrots until tender. You can boil them separately in water or roast them in the oven until they are easily pierced with a fork. Once cooked, let them cool, then peel and dice them into small cubes.

Combine the Ingredients:
- In a large mixing bowl, combine the diced beets, potatoes, carrots, chopped onion, diced dill pickle, and green peas. Mix well to combine all the ingredients evenly.

Make the Dressing:
- In a small bowl, whisk together the vegetable oil, apple cider vinegar (or white wine vinegar), Dijon mustard, salt, and pepper to make the vinaigrette dressing.

Dress the Salad:
- Pour the dressing over the salad ingredients in the mixing bowl. Gently toss to coat the vegetables with the dressing. Adjust the seasoning with more salt and pepper if needed.

Chill:

- Cover the bowl with plastic wrap or transfer the salad to an airtight container. Refrigerate for at least 1-2 hours to allow the flavors to meld together and the salad to chill.

Serve:
- Before serving, give the salad a final toss. Garnish with chopped fresh dill or parsley, if desired.
- Russian Beet Salad (Vinegret) can be served cold as a side dish or light meal. It's delicious on its own or served with crusty bread or rye crackers.

Enjoy:
- Enjoy the vibrant flavors and colors of this classic Russian salad. It's nutritious, satisfying, and perfect for sharing with friends and family.

This recipe for Russian Beet Salad (Vinegret) is customizable, and you can adjust the ingredients and seasonings according to your taste preferences. Feel free to add additional vegetables such as peas, beans, or pickles, or omit any ingredients you don't have on hand.

Russian Chicken Soup (Solyanka)

Ingredients:

- 500g chicken breasts or thighs, diced
- 200g smoked sausage or ham, sliced
- 1 onion, finely chopped
- 2 cloves garlic, minced
- 2 tablespoons vegetable oil
- 2 large potatoes, peeled and diced
- 1 carrot, peeled and diced
- 1 bell pepper, diced
- 4 cups chicken broth
- 1/2 cup dill pickles, chopped
- 1/4 cup pickle brine (liquid from the pickle jar)
- 1 tablespoon tomato paste
- 1 tablespoon capers (optional)
- 1 tablespoon olives, sliced (optional)
- 1 bay leaf
- 1 teaspoon paprika
- Salt and pepper, to taste
- Sour cream, for serving (optional)
- Chopped fresh dill or parsley, for garnish

Instructions:

Sauté the Meats and Vegetables:
- In a large pot or Dutch oven, heat the vegetable oil over medium heat. Add the diced chicken and sliced sausage or ham. Cook until the chicken is browned and the sausage or ham is lightly browned, about 5-7 minutes. Remove from the pot and set aside.
- In the same pot, add the chopped onion and minced garlic. Sauté until the onion is translucent and fragrant, about 3-4 minutes.

Add the Vegetables and Broth:
- Add the diced potatoes, carrots, and bell pepper to the pot with the sautéed onion and garlic. Cook for another 5 minutes, stirring occasionally.
- Pour in the chicken broth and bring the soup to a simmer.

Simmer the Soup:
- Add the cooked chicken and sausage or ham back to the pot. Stir in the chopped dill pickles, pickle brine, tomato paste, capers (if using), olives (if using), bay leaf, and paprika. Season with salt and pepper to taste.
- Cover the pot and let the soup simmer gently for about 20-25 minutes, or until the vegetables are tender and the flavors have melded together.

Serve:
- Ladle the hot Russian Chicken Soup (Solyanka) into bowls. Serve with a dollop of sour cream (if using) and a sprinkle of chopped fresh dill or parsley on top.
- Enjoy this hearty and flavorful soup with crusty bread or crackers on the side.

This recipe for Russian Chicken Soup (Solyanka) is versatile, and you can customize it by adding other ingredients such as mushrooms, cabbage, or different types of meats. Adjust the seasonings according to your taste preferences for a delicious and satisfying meal.

Russian Cabbage Rolls (Golubtsy)

Ingredients:

For the Cabbage Rolls:

- 1 large head of cabbage
- 500g ground beef or a mixture of beef and pork
- 1 cup cooked rice
- 1 onion, finely chopped
- 2 cloves garlic, minced
- 1 carrot, grated
- Salt and pepper, to taste
- 1 egg
- 2 tablespoons breadcrumbs (optional)
- Vegetable oil, for frying

For the Tomato Sauce:

- 2 tablespoons vegetable oil
- 1 onion, finely chopped
- 2 cloves garlic, minced
- 1 can (400g) crushed tomatoes
- 1 tablespoon tomato paste
- 1 teaspoon paprika
- 1 teaspoon sugar
- Salt and pepper, to taste
- Fresh parsley or dill, chopped, for garnish

Instructions:

Prepare the Cabbage:
- Bring a large pot of salted water to a boil. Carefully remove the core from the cabbage and immerse the whole head in the boiling water. Cook for about 5-7 minutes, until the outer leaves are tender and can be easily peeled off. Remove the cabbage from the pot and let it cool slightly. Peel

off the softened outer leaves and set them aside. Repeat the process until you have about 12-15 large leaves.

Make the Filling:
- In a large mixing bowl, combine the ground beef, cooked rice, chopped onion, minced garlic, grated carrot, salt, pepper, egg, and breadcrumbs (if using). Mix until well combined.

Assemble the Golubtsy:
- Place a cabbage leaf flat on a cutting board. Trim off the thick center stem. Spoon a portion of the filling onto the center of the leaf. Fold the sides of the leaf over the filling and roll it up tightly, tucking in the sides as you go. Repeat with the remaining cabbage leaves and filling.

Brown the Golubtsy:
- In a large skillet, heat some vegetable oil over medium heat. Place the rolled cabbage leaves seam side down in the skillet and cook until lightly browned on all sides, about 2-3 minutes per side. Remove from the skillet and set aside.

Prepare the Tomato Sauce:
- In the same skillet, heat 2 tablespoons of vegetable oil over medium heat. Add the chopped onion and minced garlic, and sauté until softened and fragrant, about 3-4 minutes. Stir in the crushed tomatoes, tomato paste, paprika, sugar, salt, and pepper. Bring the sauce to a simmer and cook for about 5 minutes, stirring occasionally.

Simmer the Golubtsy:
- Place the browned cabbage rolls back into the skillet with the tomato sauce, making sure they are snugly arranged in a single layer. Spoon some of the sauce over the top of the Golubtsy. Cover the skillet and let the cabbage rolls simmer over low heat for about 30-40 minutes, or until the filling is cooked through and the cabbage is tender.

Serve:
- Once cooked, remove the Golubtsy from the skillet and transfer them to a serving platter. Spoon some of the tomato sauce over the top and sprinkle with chopped fresh parsley or dill. Serve hot, accompanied by mashed potatoes or crusty bread.

Enjoy these delicious and comforting Russian Cabbage Rolls (Golubtsy) as a hearty main dish for a satisfying meal!

Russian Mushroom Piroshki

Ingredients:

For the Dough:

- 2 1/2 cups all-purpose flour
- 1 teaspoon active dry yeast
- 1/2 cup warm milk
- 1/4 cup warm water
- 1 tablespoon granulated sugar
- 1 egg
- 2 tablespoons vegetable oil
- 1/2 teaspoon salt

For the Filling:

- 300g mushrooms (button mushrooms or any variety you prefer), finely chopped
- 1 onion, finely chopped
- 2 cloves garlic, minced
- 2 tablespoons butter or vegetable oil
- 1 tablespoon all-purpose flour
- 1/2 cup vegetable or chicken broth
- Salt and pepper, to taste
- Chopped fresh parsley or dill, for garnish (optional)

Instructions:

Prepare the Dough:
- In a small bowl, dissolve the active dry yeast and sugar in warm water. Let it sit for about 5-10 minutes until frothy.
- In a large mixing bowl, combine the flour and salt. Make a well in the center and add the frothy yeast mixture, warm milk, egg, and vegetable oil. Mix until a soft dough forms.
- Knead the dough on a floured surface for about 5-7 minutes, until smooth and elastic. Place the dough in a greased bowl, cover with a clean kitchen towel, and let it rise in a warm place for about 1 hour, or until doubled in size.

Prepare the Filling:

- In a skillet, melt the butter or heat the vegetable oil over medium heat. Add the chopped onions and sauté until softened and translucent, about 3-4 minutes.
- Add the minced garlic and chopped mushrooms to the skillet. Cook, stirring occasionally, until the mushrooms release their moisture and begin to brown, about 5-7 minutes.
- Sprinkle the flour over the mushrooms and stir to combine. Cook for another minute to cook off the raw flour taste.
- Gradually pour in the vegetable or chicken broth, stirring constantly, until the mixture thickens into a gravy-like consistency. Season with salt and pepper to taste. Remove from heat and let the filling cool slightly.

Assemble the Piroshki:

- Preheat your oven to 375°F (190°C). Line a baking sheet with parchment paper.
- Punch down the risen dough and divide it into equal portions, depending on the size of piroshki you desire.
- Roll out each portion of dough into a circle on a floured surface. Place a spoonful of the mushroom filling in the center of each circle of dough.
- Fold the edges of the dough over the filling to enclose it completely, shaping the piroshki into a round or oval shape. Pinch the edges tightly to seal.

Bake the Piroshki:

- Place the assembled piroshki seam side down on the prepared baking sheet. Brush the tops with a beaten egg for a shiny finish (optional).
- Bake in the preheated oven for 20-25 minutes, or until the piroshki are golden brown and cooked through.

Serve:

- Remove the piroshki from the oven and let them cool slightly on the baking sheet. Garnish with chopped fresh parsley or dill, if desired.
- Serve the Russian Mushroom Piroshki warm as a delicious appetizer, snack, or side dish. They can be enjoyed on their own or with a side of sour cream or a dipping sauce.

These homemade Russian Mushroom Piroshki are sure to impress with their savory filling and golden, fluffy dough. Enjoy their delicious flavor and comforting texture straight from the oven!

Russian Cabbage Pie (Kulebyaka)

Ingredients:

For the Dough:

- 2 1/2 cups all-purpose flour
- 1 cup unsalted butter, cold and cubed
- 1/2 teaspoon salt
- 1/2 cup cold water

For the Filling:

- 1 small cabbage, shredded
- 200g mushrooms, sliced
- 1 onion, chopped
- 2 cloves garlic, minced
- 1 cup cooked rice
- 3 hard-boiled eggs, chopped
- 2 tablespoons vegetable oil
- Salt and pepper, to taste
- 1 egg, beaten (for egg wash)

Instructions:

Prepare the Dough:
- In a large mixing bowl, combine the flour and salt. Add the cold, cubed butter to the flour mixture.
- Using a pastry cutter or your fingers, work the butter into the flour until the mixture resembles coarse crumbs.
- Gradually add the cold water to the flour mixture, stirring with a fork until the dough comes together. Form the dough into a ball, wrap it in plastic wrap, and refrigerate for at least 30 minutes.

Prepare the Filling:
- In a large skillet, heat the vegetable oil over medium heat. Add the chopped onion and minced garlic, and sauté until softened and fragrant, about 3-4 minutes.
- Add the sliced mushrooms to the skillet and cook until they release their moisture and start to brown, about 5-7 minutes.

- Stir in the shredded cabbage and cook until wilted, about 5 minutes. Season with salt and pepper to taste.
- Remove the skillet from the heat and let the filling cool slightly. Once cooled, stir in the cooked rice and chopped hard-boiled eggs until well combined.

Assemble the Pie:
- Preheat your oven to 375°F (190°C). Line a baking sheet with parchment paper.
- On a lightly floured surface, roll out the chilled dough into a rectangle or oval shape, about 1/4 inch thick.
- Transfer the rolled-out dough to the prepared baking sheet. Spoon the cabbage and mushroom filling onto one half of the dough, leaving a border around the edges.
- Fold the other half of the dough over the filling to cover it completely. Press the edges together to seal and crimp with a fork to create a decorative border. Make a few slits in the top of the pie to allow steam to escape during baking.
- Brush the top of the pie with beaten egg for a golden finish.

Bake the Pie:
- Place the assembled pie in the preheated oven and bake for 35-40 minutes, or until the crust is golden brown and crispy.

Serve:
- Remove the Russian Cabbage Pie (Kulebyaka) from the oven and let it cool slightly before slicing and serving.
- Serve the pie warm as a delicious main dish or as part of a festive meal. Enjoy its savory filling and flaky pastry crust!

This homemade Russian Cabbage Pie (Kulebyaka) is sure to impress with its delicious flavor and rustic charm. Feel free to customize the filling with your favorite ingredients, such as meat or different vegetables, to suit your taste preferences.

Russian Fish Soup (Ukha)

Ingredients:

- 1 kg fish fillets (such as salmon, trout, cod, or pike), cut into chunks
- 2 liters water
- 1 onion, chopped
- 2 carrots, peeled and sliced
- 2 potatoes, peeled and diced
- 1 celery stalk, diced
- 1 leek, sliced
- 2 bay leaves
- 4-5 whole peppercorns
- Salt, to taste
- Fresh dill, chopped, for garnish
- Lemon wedges, for serving

Instructions:

Prepare the Broth:
- In a large pot, combine the water, chopped onion, sliced carrots, diced potatoes, diced celery, sliced leek, bay leaves, and whole peppercorns. Bring the mixture to a boil over medium-high heat.
- Once boiling, reduce the heat to low and let the broth simmer gently for about 20-25 minutes, or until the vegetables are tender and the flavors have melded together.

Add the Fish:
- Carefully add the fish chunks to the simmering broth. Cook for an additional 5-7 minutes, or until the fish is cooked through and flakes easily with a fork. Be careful not to overcook the fish, as it can become dry and tough.

Season and Serve:
- Season the Ukha with salt to taste. Remove the bay leaves and discard.
- Ladle the hot soup into bowls. Garnish each serving with chopped fresh dill and serve with lemon wedges on the side.

Enjoy:

- Serve the Russian Fish Soup (Ukha) hot as a comforting and nourishing meal. Enjoy its delicate flavors and hearty ingredients with crusty bread or crackers on the side.

Feel free to customize this recipe by adding other vegetables or herbs according to your taste preferences. You can also adjust the seasoning with additional herbs or spices for extra flavor. Russian Fish Soup (Ukha) is a versatile dish that can be enjoyed year-round and is perfect for sharing with family and friends.

Russian Garlic Bread (Pampushki)

Ingredients:

- 500g all-purpose flour
- 1 packet (7g) active dry yeast
- 1 cup warm milk
- 2 tablespoons sugar
- 2 tablespoons vegetable oil
- 2 cloves garlic, minced
- 2 tablespoons chopped fresh parsley
- 1 teaspoon salt
- 1 egg, beaten (for egg wash)
- Additional vegetable oil or melted butter for brushing

Instructions:

Activate the Yeast:
- In a small bowl, combine the warm milk and sugar. Sprinkle the active dry yeast over the milk mixture and let it sit for about 5-10 minutes, or until frothy.

Prepare the Dough:
- In a large mixing bowl, combine the flour, minced garlic, chopped fresh parsley, salt, and vegetable oil. Pour in the activated yeast mixture and mix until a soft dough forms.
- Turn the dough out onto a floured surface and knead for about 5-7 minutes, or until smooth and elastic.

First Rise:
- Place the dough in a greased bowl, cover with a clean kitchen towel, and let it rise in a warm place for about 1 hour, or until doubled in size.

Shape the Bread:
- Punch down the risen dough and divide it into equal-sized portions, depending on how large you want your pampushki to be. Roll each portion into a ball and place them on a parchment-lined baking sheet, leaving some space between each ball.
- Cover the baking sheet with a clean kitchen towel and let the dough balls rise for another 30-45 minutes, or until puffy.

Preheat the Oven:

- Meanwhile, preheat your oven to 375°F (190°C).

Brush with Egg Wash:
- Once the dough balls have risen, gently brush the tops with beaten egg for a shiny finish.

Bake:
- Bake the pampushki in the preheated oven for 15-20 minutes, or until golden brown on top and cooked through. You can tap the bottom of a bread roll to check if it sounds hollow, indicating it's done.

Brush with Garlic Butter:
- While the pampushki are still warm, brush the tops with additional vegetable oil or melted butter mixed with minced garlic for extra flavor.

Serve:
- Serve the Russian Garlic Bread (Pampushki) warm alongside your favorite soups or stews. Enjoy the soft and aromatic bread with its delicious garlic and herb-infused flavor.

These homemade Russian Garlic Bread (Pampushki) are perfect for dipping into soups or enjoying on their own as a tasty snack. They're sure to be a hit at your table!

Russian Potato Pancakes (Draniki)

Ingredients:

- 4 large potatoes, peeled
- 1 small onion, peeled
- 1 egg
- 2-3 tablespoons all-purpose flour
- 1 teaspoon salt
- 1/2 teaspoon black pepper
- Vegetable oil, for frying
- Sour cream, for serving (optional)
- Chopped fresh dill or parsley, for garnish (optional)

Instructions:

Grate the Potatoes and Onion:
- Using a box grater or a food processor with a grating attachment, grate the peeled potatoes and onion. Place them in a clean kitchen towel or cheesecloth and squeeze out as much liquid as possible.

Mix the Batter:
- In a large mixing bowl, combine the grated potatoes and onion with the egg, all-purpose flour, salt, and black pepper. Mix well until everything is evenly combined and the mixture holds together.

Heat the Oil:
- In a large skillet or frying pan, heat enough vegetable oil over medium heat to cover the bottom of the pan generously.

Fry the Pancakes:
- Once the oil is hot, drop spoonfuls of the potato mixture into the skillet, using the back of the spoon to flatten them into pancake shapes. Make sure not to overcrowd the pan.
- Fry the potato pancakes for 3-4 minutes on each side, or until golden brown and crispy. Use a spatula to flip them carefully.

Drain and Serve:
- Once cooked, transfer the potato pancakes to a plate lined with paper towels to drain any excess oil.

Serve:

- Serve the Russian Potato Pancakes (Draniki) hot, garnished with a dollop of sour cream and chopped fresh dill or parsley if desired. They can be enjoyed on their own or served alongside applesauce, sour cream, or smoked salmon for extra flavor.

Enjoy:
- Enjoy these crispy and flavorful Russian Potato Pancakes (Draniki) as a delicious side dish or appetizer. They're perfect for breakfast, brunch, or any time you're craving something comforting and satisfying.

These homemade Draniki are simple to make and incredibly tasty, with a crispy exterior and soft, tender interior. They're a classic dish in Russian cuisine and are sure to become a favorite in your household too!

Russian Meat Pie (Kurnik)

Ingredients:

For the Dough:

- 3 cups all-purpose flour
- 1 teaspoon salt
- 1 cup unsalted butter, cold and cubed
- 1/2 cup sour cream
- 1 egg, beaten (for egg wash)

For the Filling:

- 500g boneless chicken thighs or breasts, diced
- 200g mushrooms, sliced
- 1 onion, finely chopped
- 2 cloves garlic, minced
- 2 carrots, grated
- 1 cup cooked rice
- 1/2 cup chicken broth
- 1/2 cup sour cream
- 2 tablespoons vegetable oil
- Salt and pepper, to taste
- Chopped fresh dill or parsley, for garnish

Instructions:

Make the Dough:
- In a large mixing bowl, combine the flour and salt. Add the cold cubed butter and use a pastry cutter or your fingers to cut the butter into the flour until the mixture resembles coarse crumbs.
- Add the sour cream and mix until the dough comes together. If the dough is too dry, you can add a little cold water, one tablespoon at a time, until it reaches the right consistency.
- Shape the dough into a ball, wrap it in plastic wrap, and refrigerate for at least 30 minutes.

Prepare the Filling:
- In a large skillet, heat the vegetable oil over medium heat. Add the chopped onion and minced garlic, and sauté until softened and fragrant, about 3-4 minutes.
- Add the diced chicken to the skillet and cook until browned on all sides, about 5-7 minutes.
- Stir in the sliced mushrooms and grated carrots, and cook for another 5 minutes, until the vegetables are tender.
- Add the cooked rice and chicken broth to the skillet, and simmer for 2-3 minutes. Stir in the sour cream and season with salt and pepper to taste. Remove from heat and let the filling cool slightly.

Assemble the Pie:
- Preheat your oven to 375°F (190°C). Grease a 9-inch round baking dish or springform pan.
- Divide the dough into two portions, one slightly larger than the other. Roll out the larger portion of dough on a floured surface to fit the bottom and sides of the baking dish.
- Place the rolled-out dough in the greased baking dish, pressing it gently into the bottom and up the sides.
- Spoon the cooled filling mixture into the dough-lined baking dish, spreading it out evenly.

Cover with the Top Crust:
- Roll out the remaining portion of dough on a floured surface to fit the top of the pie. Place it over the filling, sealing the edges by pressing them together with the bottom crust.

Bake:
- Brush the top of the pie with beaten egg for a golden finish.
- Using a sharp knife, make a few slits in the top crust to allow steam to escape during baking.
- Bake in the preheated oven for 40-45 minutes, or until the crust is golden brown and the filling is bubbling.

Serve:
- Remove the Russian Meat Pie (Kurnik) from the oven and let it cool slightly before slicing.
- Garnish with chopped fresh dill or parsley before serving.
- Serve slices of the pie warm as a main dish for a festive meal or special occasion.

This Russian Meat Pie (Kurnik) is a delicious and impressive dish that's sure to be a hit at your table. Enjoy its flavorful filling and flaky crust with family and friends!

This Russian Meat Pie (Kurnik) is a delicious and impressive dish that's sure to be a hit at your table. Enjoy its flavorful filling and flaky crust with family and friends!